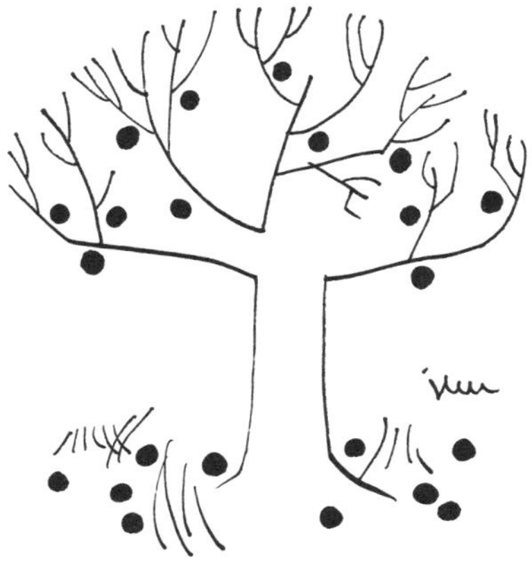

The Art of Adding and the Art of Taking Away

SELECTIONS FROM

John Updike's Manuscripts

AN EXHIBITION

AT THE HOUGHTON LIBRARY

BY ELIZABETH A. FALSEY

The Harvard College Library

Cambridge · Massachusetts · 1987

Foreword

This catalogue and exhibition attempt the unlikely task of visually depicting textual development and change. We want the reader to look at individual texts as if they were pictures, but if he can be coaxed to read a little too, that is all to the good. We won't know until later if we have had any success. Thanks, first of all, go to John Updike, for placing his manuscripts at Harvard, for permitting this exhibition, helping Miss Falsey, writing a preface to this catalogue and for having been for a long time the pride of American letters. Thanks also go to Vicki Denby for coping with text, labels, and the word processor and to Roger Stoddard who brings all of our projects to life.

Finally our warmest gratitude goes to Ronald Lee Fleming and Haven O'More, good friends who paid for this catalogue, and to a couple who would like to be anonymous, but who appeared at the end when our costs ran over.

RODNEY G. DENNIS
Curator of Manuscripts

The illustrations, from a series of drawings displayed in the exhibition, are by John Updike. Oxford and [n.p.] 1954–1955 and [n.d.]. bMS Am 1793.1 (29)

Preface to a Partial Catalogue of My Own Leavings

Coming into Cambridge last November to view the proposed contents of this exhibit, I had expected to greet old friends— yellowed manuscripts and elaborated proofsheets the sight of which, like so many retasted madeleines, would cause to well up fond memories of bygone moments and outgrown selves and faded sites, towns and houses and rooms, where I had once labored. Instead, I found myself facing a shuffled multitude of hostile strangers— aborted stories I had totally forgotten, tortuous changes that had utterly slipped my mind, old editorial tussles mercifully quite erased from recollection. Who was this writer? And what did he have to do with me? I was overswept by a panicky sense of the fundamental unseemliness of such an exhibition, such a display of the bedraggled gray underwear that literary enterprise wears beneath the plumage and silks in which it fancies itself trotting forth. The false starts, the misspellings, the factual errors, the repetitions, the downright ungrammar, the marginal chastisements severe and tender, the craven thrift and cunning with which a pitifully slender store of inspirations is hoarded and recycled— all set out in cases, like the mummified bits gathering dust in Egyptian museums, sad bits of bandage and skin and bone and once-magical embalming honey proclaiming in their abject confusion and hapless desiccation the scarcely believable fact that long ago life, human life, had passed this way and striven for perpetuation.

Some writers, like the late Vladimir Nabokov, have made a point of destroying all manuscripts and intermediate stages of their works of art, thus presenting to posterity an implacably clean face. Others, like Theodore Dreiser, have been so solicitous of their remnants as to keep carbons of even their love letters. In a less self-conscious time than ours, before authorship was seen as a means of generating academic treasure, the accidents of the printshop and the attic were allowed to carry away the smudged and frayed by-products of the making of books; combustion and careless housemaids also relieved the world of much that might now seem precious. Now, in an age unprecedented in its ability to generate "papers," an indeterminate potential value attaches itself to every scrap, and prodigies of storage and cataloguing are achieved. The egoistic fantasy that everything one does possesses great worth and interest has been, in my case, rather wickedly encouraged by the Houghton Library, which twenty years ago suggested that I deposit in the library's meticulous, humidified care the refuse of my profession.

My gratitude goes to Rodney Dennis for proffering this suggestion and putting up with its messy aftermath, and my admiration goes to Elizabeth Falsey for selecting points of interest and making coherent cases of them. I myself find other writers' drafts and worksheets fascinating; one draws closer, bending over (say) Keats' first version of "Ode to a Nightingale" in the British Museum, to the sacred flame, the furnace of mental concentration wherein a masterpiece was still ductile and yielding to blows of the pen. But inspecting such material is (like most science) a form of prying; we should not forget that what we glimpse here is the long and winding middle of a human process whose end is a *published thing*— shiny, fragrant, infinitely distributable— and whose beginning is the belief on the author's part that he or she has something to say, *something to deliver*. Both this vague initial impetus and solid end-product partake of ecstacy: however tainted and flawed the vehicles of their essence, the essence is clean and good. The creative process is lit from two directions— by the remembered flash of the first innocent and thrilling vision, and by the anticipated steady glow of the perfected, delivered result, in its crisp trimmings of manufacture. It takes strong light and high hope to bring the writer through the dreary maze of writing. Most of writing is reading— reading again, to regrasp what is there. As writers go, I am not much of a reviser, but, seeing these numerous papers spread out, I quailed at how multiple and fallible are the procedures that work toward even a straightforward text, which then when published is not safe, as long as the author lives, from further revision. And even after the author has died, in cases as worthy as those of Faulkner and Joyce, zealous scholars go on, removing alleged typos and restoring squeamishly deleted passages until no such thing as a final text seems to exist, and the very books on the shelf, though bound in vellum, have a somewhat tentative air.

My pleasure in this exhibit depends upon my sensation of detachment; its items were typed and scribbled by a series of ever-older young men whom I no longer know well, but with whom I once evidently enjoyed a close relation. On the basis of that relation I have been invited to say a word in this catalogue, which I here do, and now have done. A parable: More than once, walking on a soft and nearly unpopulated beach, I have been frightened by my own footprints behind me. They seemed left by feet much bigger than mine, and there was no escaping them. Nevertheless, I kept walking forward, the fright built into the experience along with the sun, the sand, the lapping milky-green sea, and the pink cliffs ahead, where the pelicans were dive-bombing, their own bodies the bombs.

JOHN UPDIKE

Introduction: Making and Changing the Text

Among the hundreds of feet of John Updike's papers in the Houghton Library, there is a three-by-five-inch slip of white paper on which is written, in the author's hand, in blue fountain-pen ink, probably in 1954, probably in Oxford: "writing ~~in~~ well involves two / gifts— the ~~g~~ art of ~~taking~~ / adding, and the art of taking away. / Of the two, the first is ~~most~~ more / important, since without it the / second could not exist."

The handwriting is recognizable and doesn't seem to have changed very much over thirty years; ink can be distinguished from pencil, crayon, or the typewriter. The kind of paper the words are written on is common, at least in Cambridge, in 1986— it's the kind we use in this library for notes. Its size and color can be measured and noted, and it isn't yellowed, nor does the ink seem faded. I first saw this slip of paper in a folder with draft fragments, notes, and lists of possible stories, almost all of which, in one way or another, can be dated as having been written in Oxford in 1954–1955. It seems to me that this piece is one of those fragments, but it might have been written about them, this year. The two sentences may appear, as they are or with revision, in a longer finished or unfinished piece of writing, but I don't recognize them as a fragment. The handwriting is uniform and fairly neat— I have seen manuscripts in the same hand that were probably written faster. Some words and letters on the paper are crossed out and followed, in the lines the words make on the sheet, by substitute words. The substitutions do not appear above the crossed-out words and letters, and they are in the same color of ink: I think they were made as the words were first written down. I can speculate on the nature of the substitutions: on the paper in front of me, "writing" becomes "writing well," "gift" or "giving" gives way to "art," "more" for "most" concedes a larger claim to grammar. And the passage is about something: it says, among other things, that writing is recording, that writing makes witness.

The present exhibition seeks to demonstrate with physical objects how text changes. Since 1966 John Updike has been depositing his manuscripts in the Houghton Library. He brings them, a carton or two at a time, once or twice a year, to the back door. We take them in, catalogue them, and make most of them available to the people whom we call, using the British term, readers. There are notes, sketches, drawings, plot diagrams, and drafts of novels, stories, poems, essays, pageants, plays, and speeches. Written in Elverson and Shillington Pennsylvania, Moretown Vermont, Cambridge, Oxford, London, New York, Ipswich, Georgetown, and Beverly Farms, from the early 1950s through 1986, the texts are handwritten in pen and pencil, typed, photocopied, word-processed, and in various stages of print. There are research notes and clippings, first drafts, galley and page proofs revised and annotated by Updike and others, copies of books marked up for later printings, correspondence with editors and publishers. There are examples of an early version of a single text with five or six subsequent versions, of fragments removed from one text and visibly developing into another, of a story becoming a novel or a poem becoming a story. On almost every sheet there are revisions of words or sentences. John Updike is, of course, still writing. He has always been interested in the look of both the pages on which his words are printed and the books into which they are bound. He uses opportunities offered by new printings of single texts or by collections of essays, stories, or poems to make still further changes, readjusting parts to new wholes for new readers.

Looking at changing text breaks categories— between genres, between spectator and spectacle, between disciplines. We hope that a display of some of the varied material I have described— selections from a wealth of one author's texts in the process of composition and revision— will set before a general audience some questions both about the processes of reading and writing and about the development of text. The exhibition is intended to interest a wide variety of visitors, some of them new to Houghton: specifically readers of Updike, but also scholars, critics, textual editors, bibliographers, publishers, general readers, teachers of reading and writing, anyone with a professional or personal curiosity in the psychology of reading or the psychology of writing, anyone with an interest in how things are made. The rest of this introduction will name some of the general problems raised by texts that change.

Some distinctions should be made. First, a matter of emphasis, our topic is texts malleable in the making, not in the copying. When a text is copied, by hand or by machine, changes may occur; whether they are early manuscripts or printed editions, we tend to read copies, to note their similarities and differences, in terms of their fidelity to an original complete text that precedes them. Investigation of copies seems to involve notions of decline, of accidental loss. In this exhibition, however, although we make note of a few possible instances of a misreading by a printer or an accidental reprinting of an early version of a text, we are concerned primarily with deliberate changes made by the author. Whereas with copies our attention is drawn back to an original text, with drafts and revisions our interest is engaged by hypotheses of progress, of motion toward a future, finished, stable text. Nonetheless, in the experience of looking at the notes, drafts, and revisions of a contemporary writer still very much at work, our assumption about a future moment of completeness in the moment of print (the hypothesis of a stable text) has a way of turning back on itself, giving way to other questions. Though we may anchor ourselves in the latest printed text supervised by the writer, in looking at drafts we are looking at process itself.

Second, we are concerned here with a particular American author who has earned a living in the second half of the twentieth century by writing, and we are concerned with texts of lectures, poems, novels, essays, made to be spoken on a public occasion or printed in a magazine or book. Letters, golf scores, reading notes— texts not apparently made for us— may turn up in novels; they are then, for our purposes, fragments of text for publication. And whether the observations to be made about John Updike's drafts and revisions might have something in common with observations to be made about those of other writers— whether one might construct a typology of drafts— is one of the questions the exhibit seeks to raise.

Looking at changing text raises questions about reading and about writing. The questions about writing are particular and are best addressed, as the material here displayed suggests, by examining particular texts. Reading, too, is of course always the reading of a particular text, but it may be useful at the outset to try to anticipate the experience of a reader confronted with the peculiar combination of the familiar and the strange that this exhibition presents. Looking at the process of writing is fascinating, it raises historical and critical questions, and it may be disturbing or disorienting.

Why are drafts of an author's manuscripts fascinating? First, they are evidence of *work*, and they compel attention the way a construction site compels attention. They make us acknowledge that things in the environment we might otherwise have taken for granted are artifacts, made things, and might have been made differently. Seeing that the short story "Four Sides of One Story" began as a poem and might have been a sequence of poems, or that the author checked parts of *Roger's Version* with a computer expert, or that he changed the ending of one essay in a collection so that it would not conclude with the same word as another essay— after such glimpses of the construction of texts we think we know, we are more alert in the presence of the familiar. We know that, through accident or design, things might have been, might still be, otherwise.

Made things belong to the world of fact. Drafts and revisions insist on the author's reality and on our own. The sequence of words on the paper may be beautiful or believable or neither, we may wish the words were different, but the sheet in front of us exists, and it provokes other questions, the kind associated with history or the law. Who wrote it? When? Where? The answers to such questions, the kind of minimal information we would expect to find written on a snapshot or a catalogue card, locate, name, and authenticate writing as an event. In the case of John Updike, the record is full: the handwriting of one of the *New Yorker*'s copy editors looks something like Updike's own, but it is usually easy to tell whether he has initiated or authorized a change in text. More interesting is the light that changing text throws on critical questions: information about who, when, and where can inform us about *what* a particular text is, why it is the way it is. What do drafts and revisions mean in relation to published text? to an author's intention? to a reading public's articulated preferences? to certain conventional critical categories? In the history of the different printed texts of *Rabbit, Run,* for example, besides changes in already printed text, we can see sections of text discarded from first printings returning, amplified, in later editions. These changes might be understood in terms of permission granted by different, later readers— through their representatives, the author and his publishers— for greater frankness in sexual matters. Seeing that the first notes for the first Bech story contain two lines of dialogue, or seeing the successive variations of a story in which a man tells a woman that she looks "like a voluptuous piece of wallpaper," we might conclude that the formal impulse behind the stories "The Bulgarian Poetess" and "When Everyone was Pregnant" had to do with capturing and devising a setting for spoken words. Noting, in the research that preceded the writing of the recent novels, the author's obvious concern with accuracy of reference, we might invoke words like "realism." In the middle of the draft of "Why Write?" after the author recalls that as a child he made pictures in order to capture things and connect them, there is a submerged text about a submerged text, one of the ghosts or toasters caught in the branches of *Rabbit Redux*. Updike tells us that the last sentence of that novel, "O.K.?" referred in the writing of it to the conversation of the astronauts Armstrong and Aldrin just before setting foot on the moon— a reference confirmed, not only by the epigraph to the last chapter, but also by the notes for the novel. And so on. We tend to think of both reading and writing as separate and private activities: we may imagine the ideal reader alone in his study, the ideal writer alone in his, the two in touch with each other through the medium of the ideal unchanging text in which distances of time, space, temperament disappear. Drafts and revisions confuse these two solitudes: in early drafts we see, on the page, the writer reading his own text; in revisions made in response to suggestions by family members or editors, we see, on the page, the reader's presence in the writing.

Fascinating and informative, looking at changing text may also be disorienting. Looking at a draft, seeing as fact the presence of words on the page of a piece of fiction, we are in a different relationship to the text from the one in which we stand when we read, simply, the orderly words on the bound and printed page. Pushed back from our usual connection to a stable text, looking at text that was not prepared for our eyes, we feel the customary relationships between writer and reader, words and things, fiction and fact shift slightly. There is the obvious problem, looking at a single page from the middle of a story or essay, of not knowing where we are in a text. But there are other disturbances as well.

Encountering characters we haven't met who have the names of characters we know— the Totheros of *The Plot Against Myself* or *Home*, for example—, or seeing one story break into two ("A & P" and "Lifeguard"), or simply having trouble reading the author's handwriting may be confusing, like hearing interrupted bits of music on a radio when someone else is turning the dial. In selecting items for this exhibition a choice was made to admit, even emphasize, the strangeness of looking at drafts. We have decided to show not successive versions of a few texts but stages and kinds of changes in many texts in the hope that the recognitions provoked might themselves be informative about the processes of reading and writing.

We have also resisted the pull toward displaying mainly items in various stages of print (revised galleys, for example, where the fact of change is visually more dramatic than in autograph manuscript drafts). Nonetheless, items displayed here are asking to be *read*, compared with each other and with other versions of themselves. Before turning to the exhibition cases, then, it may be helpful to address the tension between seeing and reading.

How do drafts teach us to see text? We look, first, the way a child might look at a picture book, simply, with curiosity, from a distance, without knowing what to look for: a page with marks on it. The marks have a kind of order to them; they are grouped in sequences with spaces. They may form lines which are arranged approximately parallel to each other. From the look of the marks or the paper they are written on, we may recognize this page as fitting with other pages we have seen, part of the same thing, perhaps, or written at the same time. There may be a portion of the page, where the marks are denser or of different kinds or shapes or colors, which draws attention. We might think: there something is happening. We might then return our attention to the more uniform parts of the page and think: something is happening there, too.

Now, from the look of the handwriting(s), the medium, the paper, we might want to begin grouping parts of one text together or assigning a chronological sequence to successive drafts of one poem. We could do either from the look of the pages, but how to proceed? With what assumptions? Should we suppose, for example, that the page with the highest degree of visual orderliness is early or late?

When we begin to read, we might or might not find we recognize some of the words as "fitting" with something else we have already read. If we don't recognize the words: what are they? Part of something else? Are these words an earlier version of a text we know, or part of it, or discards from it, or revisions of it? Can we tell, from a page of prose, whether we are reading part of a short story or part of a novel, and, if so, with what clues are we operating? Where there is change, either in the form of revisions "happening" on a page or in the form of two different versions of the same text, is there a pattern to the changes? Do we expect changes at formal moments, beginnings and endings of stories, say, or at moments of stress or rhyme in poems? Do we expect them around referential moments, occasioned by certain themes or topics? What conclusions can we draw— always the case is a particular one— from the evidence of a passage being reworked or not, or from the presence on the page of other hands? Can we relate one text to another? Can we tell how something began?

When we stand farther back again, there are questions about what we do *not* see. Are there pages or stages of the written record that we do not have or that have not survived? Can we infer, from what we do have, written stages that we do not have? And, even when we think we have all the written stages, what of the process of making that is "off the record"?

Keeping in mind that more happened than got recorded, and that the record in front of us is probably incomplete, we can begin to ask of a particular text: why is it the way it is? Where did it come from? What are its boundaries? Which elements in it were essential and which accidental? Why were particular changes made? To what pressures— of memory, imagination, curiosity, habit, language, genre, audience, information, context— did the text accommodate?

The questions changing texts raise for readers and the questions they enable us to ask and sometimes answer about writing come together, finally, as questions about recognition and form. In drafts, we, as readers, witness a text becoming the thing we know. When we can name a novel, story, or poem— or simply recognize a genre— from a fragment, a line or two in front of us, we are recognizing the fragment as part of a whole. Looking at drafts and revisions, we, working backwards, meet the author moving towards us, working to shape the parts and the whole toward the text in which he too, when he is finished, can recognize something as itself.

The Manuscripts

The manuscripts in this exhibition are selected to suggest the kinds of inquiry they might sustain when the exhibition is over and their full texts can be read. We have tried to let the objects themselves suggest their own grouping, but our categories are rough: any particular item might have appeared in a number of our cases. In the following pages, eleven groups of manuscripts are named and discussed briefly, and the items chosen for exhibition within each group are listed and identified.

ABBREVIATIONS

A.	autograph
MS.	manuscript
TS.	typescript
[n.p.]	no place
[n.d.]	no date
p.	page[s]
s.	sheet[s]

I
Notes and Excerpts on Writing and Reading

Our first case contains random selections of texts on writing and reading. Some are chosen from the author's notes to himself on slips or scraps of paper of the sort one might keep visible on a desk or tacked to a wall. There is one curiosity, a draft used as evidence in a law suit. And there are passages excerpted from draft versions of more formal public writing. The choice for the last group was difficult. Updike has written a lot about writing— in reviews, prefaces to his own collections and later or special editions, forewords to books by other writers, interviews, and the Bech stories. The items here were chosen partly because they themselves exemplify different stages of changing text— from first notes to marked galleys— and because they demonstrate some of the problems of displaying and briefly citing this kind of material. The passage from "Leaves" is shown in the case in both a page of draft and a revised galley. The exchange cited below between Bech and the Bulgarian poetess differs slightly from the lines in the story collected in *Bech: A Book.* The dialogue between Miss Prynne and Thomas Marshfield, implied by juxtaposing in the exhibition an early note and a page of draft, does not happen like this in *A Month of Sundays.* The second passage cited from the talk "Why Write?" is from lines crossed out in the draft, probably not spoken when the speech was delivered, and not published in the printed version in *Picked-Up Pieces.* These items provide an occasion to explain that in the entries in this catalogue, quotations are from one or more of the manuscripts in the cases: the words are often different from those in the first, second, or third published version of the text with which readers may be familiar, though they may be sufficiently like as to be recognizable. No attempt is made here to give a printing history of the text displayed, other than by indicating its final title when the item does not identify itself.

1

"Through the Mirror," later "The Bulgarian Poetess"

"Poetry difficult?"
"It is difficult to write."

An exchange between two writers: note and first page of an early draft fragment of the first story about a writer who has difficulties writing, named, in a later draft, Henry Bech. A.MS. and TS. with A.MS. revisions; [n.p.] Dec 1964 and [n.d.]. *80M-11 (993)

2

A Month of Sundays

Miss Prynne: *Now here is a sermon to be preached!*

The Rev. Thomas Marshfield: *You are yet the end, the* intelligens entis, *of my being, in so far as I exist on paper.*

The narrator addresses his reader, who has annotated a page of his journal. Notes and page from an early draft of the novel whose protagonist is writing "for therapy." A.MS. and TS. with A.MS. revisions; [n.p., n.d.]. *75M-53 (1009) s.53; *75M-53 (1008) s.193

3

"Suzie Cream Cheese Speaks"

Drafts and galleys of a 1976 book review admitted into evidence in a Los Angeles 1982 libel suit against Updike and *The New Yorker.*

A particular case of writing as recording: about the word "swindler," the author testified that *"If it was not the first word that occurred to me, it was the first right word that occurred to me."*

TS., TS. (photocopy), and galley sheets with A.MS. and MS. revisions and annotations; Ipswich and New York, 1976. *86M-3 (1)

4

[Untitled scraps and fragments]

All but the first *86M -3 (2)

A piece of humorous writing should have the texture of a cartoon.
A.MS. notes; Cambridge, 1952. *80M-11 (1051) s.1

Writing well involves two gifts— the art of adding, and the art of taking away. Of the two, the first is more important, since without it the second could not exist.
A.MS.; [Oxford, 1954–1955].

. . . the good writer is not an attractive person
A.MS.; [n.p., ca. 1956].

. . . I am conscious of being a gradually perceived wing (with perhaps a garage) on the John Updike who gets so many things in The NYer.
A.MS.; [n.p., ca. 1956].

For five full years now, though I am only 27, I have been engaged, to earn a living, in the steady production of lies.
Notes for a Diary. TS.; [n.p., 1959].

Writing is work: *don't forget it.*
A.MS.; [n.p., n.d.].

important point: surprise the reader with too little, rather than make him author-conscious with too much.
A.MS.; [n.p., n.d.].

$$\frac{\textit{prose}}{\textit{exigencies of narrative}} = \frac{\textit{poetry}}{\textit{exigencies of form}}\ ?$$

A.MS.; [n.p., n.d.].

"It is only those who half know a thing that write about it." P of BE, p. 146.
Truth— the raw, naked truth. Fanny Hill.
A.MS. and TS.; [n.p., n.d.].

We renew ourselves through effort and love
A.MS.; [n.p., n.d.].

5

"Leaves"

And what are these pages but leaves? Why do I produce them but to thrust, by some subjective photosynthesis, my guilt into nature, where there is no guilt?

TS. of the short story, with A.MS. revisions; [n.p., n.d.]. *New Yorker* galley with A.MS. and MS. annotations and revisions; New York and Ipswich, 1962. *75M-53 (1042) and bMS Am 1793.1 (25) item 20

6

"Boyhood," later "Boyhood, Mine"

The picture of myself at home; look at for some sign of congratulation, see none— what he wanted: to write or draw, to make the NYer, *to work my own hours.*

A.MS. notes for an autobiographical essay; [n.p.] Apr 1960. bMS Am 1793.1 (3)

7

"Why Write?"

. . . I would draw on one sheet of paper an assortment of objects— flowers, animals, stars, toasters, chairs, comic strip characters, ghosts, hoses— and connect them with lines, indeed a path of two lines, so that they all became the fruit of a single impossible tree.

. . . not one reader of my last novel [Rabbit Redux] *that I have talked to had realized the to me supremely obvious reference of the closing sentence, "O.K.?" The reference was to the astronautical jargon, . . .*

TS. with A.MS. revisions of a talk delivered in Adelaide, South Australia; 1974. *86M-3 (3) ss. 6 and 8 (crossed-out lines)

II
Poems

Case II contains drafts and revisions of poems, texts small enough for us, as readers, to see around, and small enough that they might first "happen" to the writer all at once. In a draft of an interview with Helen Vendler for *The New York Times Book Review* (*83M-3 [31], not displayed), Updike writes that "I would know I had one [a poem], the idea of it, when my scalp crawled. When the skin of my head felt tight. My hand would shake and I couldn't write fast enough." One way to think about revisions is in terms of circles of readers, with the author as his own first reader. The versions of "Call" demonstrate the writer's first attempt to "write fast enough" and then, after reading, to revise in light of first intention. The versions of one line of "The Amoeba," on the other hand, illustrate a technique of reworking a portion of text: revising something, not by annotating the written words, but by repeatedly rewriting like a musician going over and over a difficult passage until he gets it right. The changes in "Vacuum Cleaner" incidentally demonstrate change made in a previously printed text. The connection suggested here by putting an early untitled note for a poem about a pepper plant beside the much later poem "Query," whose first line is "Pear tree, why blossom?" is perhaps the most unorthodox in the exhibition. It is intended to raise questions about textual boundaries, about how to understand where the making of a particular text begins, and it is meant to recall the passages on leaves and impossible trees in Case I.

8

"Evening Call" / "Summer Evening Call" / "Call"

Across what green distances does this my voice

First and third drafts of a poem about calling a son home. A.MS. and TS. with A.MS. revisions; Ipswich, [May]–Sep 1964. *80M-11 (944)

9

[Untitled note] and "Inquest," later "Query"

Poem about pepper plant   Growing to what purpose? Lovely to what end?

Peartree, why blossom?

A.MS. note; [n.p., ca. 1956]. With drafts, A.MS. and TS. with A.MS. revisions, of a poem written eighteen years later; [n.p.] May and Oct 1974. bMS Am 1793.1 (28) and *86M-3 (4)

10

"The Amoeba"

Suffixes swarmed . . .

Early draft of the poem, with numerous versions of stanza 3. A.MS. and TS. with A.MS. revisions; Ipswich, May 1966. *80M-11 (939)

11

"Vacuum Cleaner" in "A Cheerful Alphabet of Pleasant Objects"

This cleaner with more ease than some

This humming broom

Of this small poem on the letter "V" (in a sequence of poems on letters of the alphabet written for the author's son David), only the title is unchanged in a series of rewritings and new printings. Early version and printer's copy for *Carpentered Hen,* Harper & Brothers, 1958. TS. with A.MS. revisions, TS. with MS. revision; [n.p., n.d.]. Marked copy of *Hoping for a Hoopoe* (the English title of the collection) and two sets of galleys indicating revisions made for *Carpentered Hen,* Knopf, 1982. bMS Am 1793.1 (9), 1793.1 (4) s. 87, and *86M-3 (5)

III
Leftovers: Early Unfinished and Unpublished Texts

The next three cases raise questions about longer texts and about genre. "Leftovers" is the word Updike wrote on a folder containing unpublished material, some of which had served as a quarry for later published writing. Case III contains a story that, much reworked, became "Pigeon Feathers." Also displayed are other unpublished texts, primarily about what in "Why Write?" the author calls "the mysterious life we led before we became writers." In these early novels, he is learning how to write novels, and he is working with the material of memory. Three are set in Pennsylvania and one in New England; some characters, situations, places are recognizable looking back from *The Centaur,* "Flight" and various Olinger stories, even from as far away as *The Coup* or *Roger's Version*.

12

The Plot Against Myself

Annie—If you will, try and get this published [Morris H. Tothero, retired supervising principal of Willow, Pennsylvania, Public Schools]

Note and draft fragment of an unfinished, unpublished novel, written in the back of a commonplace book begun in Oxford. A.MS.; [Elverson, ca. 1955]. *86M-3 (6) and bMS Am 1793.1 (12)

13

Consider the Lillies / *An Old-fashioned Romance* / *Tarzan and Jane*

All innocence, I walked down a diagonal path . . .

Aren't your feet cold?

Notes, sketches, and 8 versions of the beginning of an unfinished, unpublished novel about two Harvard undergraduate Fine Arts majors: a black student from New Jersey and the daughter of a Cambridge minister. A.MS. and TS. with A.MS. revisions; Ipswich [n.d.] and 1961. *86M-3 (7)

14

Home

Will she lose farm? / *Daddy a saint*

Pages from a plot diagram and draft of an unpublished autobiographical novel about a family in Willow, Pennsylvania in the 1940s. Characters' names reappear in later work (Tothero in *Rabbit, Run,* Hanema in *Couples*); episodes and situations are recognizable in *The Centaur,* some of the "Olinger" stories, and later autobiographical essays. A.MS. and TS. with A.MS. revisions; [New York, n.d.]. bMS Am 1793.1 (8)

15

John

Novel— John *based on texts; theme of man who gives his life to one idea*

A.MS. note (on a Church program) for an unwritten novel; New York, 1956. *86M-3 (8)

16

Go Away / *Carry Me*

Hearts with little slogans: CARRY ME, LOVE YOU, TWO AS ONE, FORGET NOT etc.

A.MS. and TS. note and draft (TS. with A.MS. revisions) of an unpublished novel about students at Olinger High School; [n.p., n.d.]. bMS Am 1793.1 (7)

17

"If the Salt have Lost his Savour"

make clearer: On the Saturday afternoon after the minister told David that there was no such thing as immortality, . . .

An unpublished story, later reworked as "Pigeon Feathers." TS. with A.MS. revisions; [Oxford and Elverson, 1955]. *86M-3 (9)

IV
Using Leftovers

Cases IV and V contain examples, not simply of recurring themes, images, or preoccupations, but of particular, already written text being used or reworked in new compositions. The connections among the texts in these cases are difficult to display simply: they ask to be read through and compared as wholes. It is relevant that many of these drafts are written on backs of typescripts of other texts. This fact reinforces the reader's sense of increasing layers, of the finished stories behind the stories, of the imaginative landscape in which new texts develop. Displayed in case IV is the opening sentence of *N + 1*, an unfinished, unpublished novel by John Updike, with a typescript of the short story "The Music School," whose narrator, himself a writer, quotes the sentence and goes on to describe the plot of his own unwritten novel. Also shown are two stories made from one: the last third of the original text of the short story "A & P," in which the narrator/clerk, goes to the beach hoping to see the girls for whose sake he has gotten himself fired, has been reworked as "Lifeguard," a meditative sermon by a divinity student/lifeguard. Updike himself has discussed some of the connections among the "Wallpaper" texts in the preface to the limited edition of *Couples: A Short Story,* printed years after the story had been written, rejected, set aside, and finally amplified without rereading into the novel of the same title. Displayed here are pages from a series of five related texts: a man who is blind in one eye— to whom everything looks flat— tells a woman in a flowered dress across the room that she looks like "a voluptuous piece of wallpaper." The first short story including his words to her was written in 1959; the last was written in 1971. In between, there was a series of unpublished stories developing from the early story, the texts of all of these so interrelated that one of the author's notes to himself (not shown) is headed simply "Y V etc." The four-sided diagram shown here on the geometry of the relationships in "Couples" is also discussed in the preface to that story.

18

"Take, Eat," later "The Music School"

The title of the book was to be "N + 1"; its first sentence went . . .

New Yorker printer's copy of a story in which the narrator refers to his unwritten novel. TS. with A.MS. revisions and MS. annotations; [New York and Ipswich] 1963. bMS Am 1793.7 (201)

An earlier draft, *80M-11 (1016), of this story quotes the first paragraph of *N + 1.*

19

N + 1

As Echo passed overhead, he stroked Maggy John's side through her big-flowered dress.

One of 5 versions of the beginning of Updike's unfinished novel. TS. with A.MS. revisions and annotations; [Ipswich, n.d.]. *86M-3 (10)

20

"A & P"

. . . they have nothing to do but have forgotten how to sleep.

New Yorker printer's copy, indicating where the original story, whose narrator is a cashier in a grocery store, was cut to make a new ending. TS. with MS. and A.MS. annotations and revisions; New York and Ipswich, Jul and Aug 1960. bMS Am 1793.1 (25) item 1

21

"Lifeguard"

They are idle, and have lost the gift of sleep . . .

Note and third version of a new story, narrated by a divinity student with a summer job, using some of the material cut from "A & P." A.MS. and TS. with A.MS. revisions; Ipswich, Aug 1960. bMS Am 1793 (41) and bMS Am 1793.1 (25) item 21

22

"You Voluptuous Piece of Wallpaper, You"

Notes and three versions of a short story never submitted for publication. TS. and TS. (carbon copy) with A.MS. revisions; Ipswich, 1959 and [n.d.]. *86M-3 (11)

23

"Couples"

. . . "like a voluptuous piece of wallpaper"

Notes for and draft of the short story, rejected in 1963 by *The New Yorker* and eventually printed in a limited edition (Halty Ferguson, 1976) with a foreword by the author discussing some of the texts here displayed. A.MS. and TS. with A.MS. revisions; Ipswich, May 1963. Draft is written on the verso of other texts, including fragments of "Four Sides of One Story." *80M-11 (995)

V
Using Leftovers, Changing Genres

Manuscripts assembled in Case V demonstrate that the story "Four Sides of One Story" and the poem "Report of Health" have a common ancestor in one poem, "Tristan" or "Letter to a Friend." The poem was finished, a fair copy was made, and then— from the evidence of these drafts— it began to change. To read these sequences of drafts, even without the author's essay on De Rougemont in the background, is to watch a text developing and changing according to an internal formal logic that recalls the "Couples" diagram in the previous case. In the sequence of texts that ends with "Four Sides of One Story," the logic dictates connectedness: Tristan implies Iseult, Iseult splits in two, these three move into prose and imply Mark; four letters are written by four characters at a formally necessary distance from one other, two of them are addressing each other, the other two are addressing outsiders. In the series of poems that ends with "Report of Health," there is movement toward inwardness and separateness: a letter that is a soliloquy. A second example of change in genre in this case is provided by Knopf galleys of a chapter of the novel *The Centaur*, marked for revision as a short story. Changes are made here to enable the excerpt to stand on its own, to adjust its diction to *New Yorker* standards, and also— an indication of the history of the text of the novel— to avoid repeating for the same readers a passage that had come from another story.

24

"Peggy's Clothes" / "Judith's Clothes"

. . . like "a voluptuous piece of wallpaper."

4 versions of a section of "Couples" retaining the line, reworked as a shorter story that was rejected by *The Saturday Evening Post* in 1966. TS. and TS. (carbon copy) with A.MS. revisions; Ipswich, Dec 1963–Oct 1966. *80M-11 (1006)

25

"Hen is Plowing Now," later "Harv is Plowing Now"

. . . ribbons of visible white that unravel again and again, always in the same direction, like a typewriter carriage

Draft and galleys of a story written in October 1963, in which an image for breaking surf is salvaged from "Couples." TS. and *New Yorker* galleys with A.MS. revisions; Ipswich, 1963–1966. *80M-11 (1004)

26

"When Everyone was Pregnant"

". . . like a voluptuous piece of wallpaper . . ."

Notes for, fragment and two versions of a short story whose narrator reminisces about the fifties; finished in June 1971 and accepted by *The New Yorker*. The sound of footsteps on a gravel driveway also survives from earlier texts. A.MS., TS., and TS. (carbon copy) with A.MS. revisions; Ipswich, 1971. *86M-3 (12)

[Not shown]

Marry me: A Romance

Their puzzling mixture of thrift and extravagance . . .

In Chapter III of the 1966 novel (whose first two chapters are revised versions of the previously published stories "Warm Wine" and "The Wait") some "Couples" material is reused. *80M-11 (1076–1086)

27

"Letter to a Friend" / "Tristan" /
"Letter to a Friend" / "Health" /
"To a Friend" / "Report of Health"

The wrong I have done you . . .

Notes for and successive versions of one poem, parts of which were reworked as the first section, a letter from Tristan to Iseult, in the short story "Four Sides of One Story." One draft of the final version of the poem, published as "Report of Health," is written on the verso of a TS. fragment of the review of De Rougemont, "More Love in the Western World." A.MS., TS. and TS. (carbon copy) with A.MS. revisions; [v.p.] 1962–1963. *80M-11 (969) and (973) and *86M-3 (13)

28

"Four Sides of One Story"

Forgive me, I seem to be on a boat

Versions of the Tristan section of the story. TS., TS. (carbon copy) with A.MS. revisions; Ipswich and New York, 1963–1965. *80M-11 (1002) and bMS Am 1793.8

VI
Beginnings: Invention and Occasions

Case VI is intended to indicate how some texts got started, to raise questions about how the origin of a text affects its shape, and to illustrate some beginnings. Some essays begin in collaboration: a suggestion to or assignment by an editor is followed by research by the author and others. Some stories (and many of Updike's poems) begin with the reading of a newspaper article. The writer keeps lists of ideas for poems, stories, novels. The first and last words of a story may be worked out before the rest of the text is written.

29

"Iseult the Fair" / "Iseult of the White Hands" / ["Iseult"]

I wanted to be sensible: to get
The damn divorce. I would
Have flown to Alabama by myself

He married me, he tells me, as a pun

I yearned to grow fat in his arms and sleep

. . . enlarged our love at our expense

Unfinished drafts of a poem, later reworked into two sections of "Four Sides of One Story." The two voices of abandoned wife and abandoned mistress differentiate in the later drafts of the poem. In the drafts here, Mark's letter exists only in prose. A.MS.; Ipswich, 1962–1963. *80M-11 (1002)

30

"More Love in the Western World"

Their passion secretly wills its own frustrations . . .

June 1963 draft of the *New Yorker* review discussing courtly love. TS. with A.MS. revisions; Ipswich, 1963. *80M-11 (1035) ss. 4 and 28

31

"On the Way to School"

My father and my mother were talking.

New Yorker printer's copy: galleys set for *Centaur* section II with MS. annotations by William Maxwell and others, and A.MS. revisions turning the chapter into the short story that appeared before the book was published; New York and Ipswich, 1962. bMS Am 1793.1 (25) item 26.

One paragraph of the novel is deleted from this story because it had previously appeared in *The New Yorker* in "Blessed Man of Boston, My Grandmother's Thimble, and Fanning Island."

32

"Baseball schedules" and "Moon"

From: Shawn.
Want to try it as an original?

New Yorker memos to and from William Shawn concerning "Talk of Town" pieces; New York, 1957. With A.MS. notes about the moon. *86M-3 (16)

33

[Untitled fragments, notes, and lists for poems, stories, novels]

Pigeons— nervous breakdown

the little social world protecting one from eternity : make COUPLES a poem?

Includes list of names of the Maples family, notes for "Pigeon Feathers," "Phenomena," "Sublimating," "The Red Herring Theory," "The Gun Shop," "Incest," three Bech stories, "The Tarbox Police," "Leaf Season," "Beautiful Husbands." A.MS. and TS. with A.MS. annotations; [v.p.] 1960–1986. *86M-3 (14)

34

[Untitled note] and "A Madman"

1. apartment search in Oxford, long train of events

TS. and A.MS. list of eight story ideas; [n.p., n.d.]. With TS. and A.MS. draft of a short story; [n.p., n.d.]. *86M-3 (17) and bMS Am 1793.1 (25) item 22

35

"Ride"

He disguised himself as a cab driver in Amman to find out what the people thought of their ruler.

Boston Globe clipping, draft (TS. with A.MS. revisions), and revised *New Yorker* page proof of the story; New York and Ipswich, 1972. *86M-3 (15)

36

"Home perhaps a meaningless tale," later "Home"

Rain in Liverpool, & two girls (harlots?) singing "— — —" under a raincoat held above their heads.

The penciled notes, themselves reworked, include the first and last words of the story. In successive versions the girls are singing "It's a Long Way to Tipperary" and "Don't Sit Under the Apple Tree." A.MS. notes, first draft, and *New Yorker* galley; [n.p., n.d.] and 1960.
bMS Am 1793.1 (25) item 17

VII
Circles of Readers: Early Readers and Editors

Case VII demonstrates some revisions made to accommodate suggestions by early readers of the manuscripts. Inconsistencies and matters of diction or information are noted by members of the author's family and other first readers. William Maxwell of *The New Yorker* suggests cuts and revisions, mainly stylistic, in "Pigeon Feathers." *New Yorker* checkers comb through galleys of stories as well as essays to verify factors and correct spellings.

37
"Pigeon Feathers"

How about leaving this to Faulkner?

Bill: on this cut, I beg a second look . . .

New Yorker printer's copy of the story, TS. with annotations in the hands of a "checker", William Maxwell, the author, and unidentified others. Ipswich and New York, Apr–Jun 1960. bMS Am 1793.1 (25) item 31

38
"Separating"

dance / art (dancing is for smaller kids)

New Yorker galley of the story, with MS. annotations in the hand of Mary (Pennington) Updike; New York and Ipswich, 1975. *86M-3 (19)

39
"Our Far-flung Correspondents: Hub Fans Bid Kid Adieu"

However: it didn't vanish . . .

New Yorker galleys of the essay with MS. annotations by "checker" and A.MS. revisions; New York and Ipswich, 1960. Facts and statistics have been checked with "Red Sox Info." With Fenway Park program, 28 Sep 1960, including A.MS. notes. bMS Am 1793.1 (25) item 27

40
"Packed Dirt, Church Going, a Dying Cat, a Traded Car"

This was checked with four Aquinas scholars . . .

Doesn't one of the Scholastics assert God made the world in play?

New Yorker galley with A.MS. revisions and annotations, and MS. annotations in the hand of a "checker" and William Maxwell; New York and Ipswich, May–Jun 1961. *86M-3 (18)

41
"God Speaks"

I do not understand who the hell changed this ī to ï. Since I made the name up, surely I am the authority

New Yorker galleys of the story with A.MS. revisions and annotations, and MS. annotations in the hands of "checkers," William Maxwell, and others; New York and Ipswich, 1965. With draft of the story. *80M-11 (1003)

42
[The Coup]: Suggestions

p.1, l.8—phrase: "crushed in *immemorial pestles"—*

MS. in the hand of Martha (Bernhard) Updike with annotations in John Updike's hand; [n.p., n.d.]. *80M-11 (1059)

43
Roger's Version

Does he say anything wrong?

Pages from a word-processed draft of the novel, annotated by the author and by Michael L. Dertouzos, who reviewed the sections about computers; Beverly Farms and Cambridge, 1985. *86M-3 (27)

VIII
Gathering Information: Research

Case VIII shows the writer himself gathering information for some of his later novels and for the second collection of Bech stories. The Rabbit books demonstrate the kind of formal pull one text can exert on another. The two sequels follow *Rabbit, Run* not just in terms of characters, settings, or diction but also in terms of the writer's and reader's expectations about what a Rabbit book should be. A standard was set in the first book— for which Updike revised proofs to include the latest popular songs— of fidelity to the present world of information. From the acknowledgements page of *The Coup* readers would know some of the sources consulted in the writing of that novel; we display a few others here. Research on witchcraft preceded the writing of *The Witches of Eastwick;* shown here are some other sources of information for that novel, including a letter from the author's daughter advising on just what radio station ought to play in the background of one scene.

44

Rabbit Redux

Toward me a little bit. Down. Okay. Now you're clear.

The events of the novel take place during the space flight; excerpts from the astronauts' conversations form chapter epigraphs. A.MS. and TS. notes on Aldrin and Armstrong's conversation of 20 Jul 1969; [n.p., n.d.].

With A.MS. notes on linotype sorts tray, clippings, and other printed material. *76M-76 (307)

45

The Coup

Drought threatens the Tuareg world

A.MS. notes; [n.p., n.d.]. With author's copy of *National Geographic*, clippings, and additional material. *80M-11 (1058)

46

Rabbit is Rich

The car sells itself— R. thinks

A.MS. notes on photocopied pages of *The Automobile Dealer*, ch. I: "The Dealer— His Purpose and Function"; [Georgetown, 1979–1980]. With photocopy of an Ann Landers clipping and other material. *81M-51 (689)

47

Bech is Back

Treyf . . . Unclean

Letters to Updike from Jacob Neusner and Michal Herzog, 1981, discussing the last words of the last of the Bech stories, "White on White." With list in Updike's hand of other books with title of Bech's first novel, for note to "Three Illuminations in the life of an American Author." *86M-3 (20)

48

Witches of Eastwick

WHJY FM— most conspicuous rock station, which is what you want, right?

Letter from Elizabeth Updike, Providence, Oct 1982. With 1982 letter from Richard Oldenburg on Niki de Saint-Phalle, copy of a 1983 letter from Updike to Judith Jones of Knopf, and notes in Updike's hand on witches and on cello-playing. *83M-3 (21)

IX
Later Readers: Collections and Changes in Previously Published Texts

Case IX shows a few examples of changes in previously published texts. Not included here are extensive revisions of single texts, like the 1974 edition of *The Poorhouse Fair*. The process of selecting texts for a collection is itself a kind of new making: Updike has referred often— in "Why Write?" for example— to the aesthetic impulse at work in making "sets" of things. Collections of stories, whether they form a sequence about the same characters, like the Bech collections or *Too Far to Go*, or are simply an assembling of recent stories, like *The Same Door*, make an occasion for revision. For *Hugging the Shore*, a collection of previously printed essays revised for this new setting, there is a list of revisions for a second edition. The text of *Rabbit is Rich* is adjusted for English readers. Most of the items in this case show text being revised in galleys or in pasted-up pages from earlier printings, but there is one example of the new technology: a paragraph from a book review that had stayed on the disc of a word processor, to be revised for inclusion in a later introduction.

49

The Same Door

. . . purple ghosts shuddered in the corners . . .

Uncut page proofs of "A Trillion Feet of Gas," with MS. and TS. revisions for the Fawcett Crest edition of this collection of stories; [New York, 1959]. bMS Am 1793.7 (180)

The collection now in print contains the unrevised text. Further revisions were made to some of the stories for the Vintage 1964 *Olinger Stories*.

50

Rabbit is Rich

Malaysia's deputy prime minister (unpronounceable) . . .

TS. with A.MS. revisions: drafts and final text for a revision in the Deutsch edition of the novel; Georgetown, 1982. *86M-3 (23)

51

Bech is Back

He had his friends, his fans, even his collectors.

Printer's copy: photocopies of printed pages of *Three Illuminations in the Life of an American Author* (from Targ edition of the *New Yorker* story) and "Bech Third-Worlds It" (from *Playboy*), pasted up and revised for the Knopf collection. Knopf galleys and page proofs show additional revisions.

Photocopy (with A.MS. and TS. revisions) and galleys with A.MS., MS., and TS. revisions; [n.p., ca. 1981]. *86M-3 (22)

52

Hugging the Shore

The Poon's function as a club and perpetuator of Brahmin tradition . . .

Pages from the printer's copy of this collection of previously published pieces, including photocopies and (as here) cut galleys pasted up with A.MS. and TS. revisions and MS. annotations in various hands; [New York and Beverly Farms] 1982–1983. With copies of two 1983 letters to Knopf, one suggesting a late change in text to avoid having two essays conclude with the same word, the other suggesting revisions for the next edition. *86M-3 (24)

53

"Out of the Evil Empire" / "Back in the U.S.S.R." / "Introduction"

Yuri Trifonov had emerged, in the last decade of his rather short life . . .

Paragraph from a *New Yorker* book review drafted on a word processor in 1984 and published in 1985, then revised on the word processor in 1985 for introduction to the Simon & Schuster edition of Trifonov's *Another Life* / *House on the Embankment*. Word-processed text and *New Yorker* galleys with A.MS. revisions; [Beverly Farms, 1984–1985]. *86M-3 (25)

X
Manuscripts of Recent Novels

This case contains, simply, drafts of recent novels: *The Coup, Rabbit is Rich, The Witches of Eastwick*, and *Roger's Version*.

54

Rabbit is Rich

Running out of gas, Rabbit thinks,

Draft, A.MS. and TS. with A.MS. revisions; Georgetown, 1978–1980. *81M-51 (690)

55

The Coup

My land of Kush, though bigger than any nation of Europe, is small for Africa, and a thousand miles from any sea.

A.MS. of early draft of chapter I; Ipswich, 28 Jan 1977. *80M-11 (1053)

My country of Kush, landlocked between the mongrelized, neo-capitalist puppet states of Zanj and Sahel, is small for Africa, though larger than any two nations of Europe.

Draft, A.MS. and TS. with A.MS. revisions; Ipswich, finished 8 Dec 1977. *80M-11 (1054)

56

The Witches of Eastwick

I. (The coven)?

First draft of the novel, A.MS. and TS. and printout with A.MS. revisions and annotations; Beverly Farms, 13 Sep 1982–15 Feb 1983. *86M-3 (28)

i. The coven

Second draft, TS. and printout with A.MS. revisions and MS. annotations; [Beverly Farms; completed 17 Feb 1983]. *86M-3 (29)

57

Roger's Version

I have been happy at the divinity school.

Draft of the novel finished 4 June 1985. A.MS. and TS. with A.MS. revisions; Beverly Farms, 1984–1985. *86M-3 (26)

XI
Rabbit, Run: Making and Changing the Text

Around the room, in the vertical cases, are a few selections from various stages in the history of one text: *Rabbit, Run*. Assembled here are a poem and two early stories— one published, one not— which may have something of the same relationship to the novel as "If the Salt have Lost his Savour" has to "Pigeon Feathers." Also displayed are some of the author's notes for the first draft and for revisions, some discarded pages, and various documents and marked galleys, proofs, and copies of printed books which illustrate the complicated printing history of the novel.

58

"Flick", later "Ace in the Hole"

I find it hard to define the effect—A picture of ordinary, "every-day" damnation?

Annotation by Albert Joseph Guerard on short story, about a former High School basketball player, submitted for Harvard English class Jb. TS. with MS. annotations in Guerard's hand and subsequent A.MS. revisions; Cambridge, Mass. and Oxford, [1953–1955?]. bMS Am 1793.1 (25) item 2

The protagonist's name in this version is the same as that of the ex-basketball player in the poem below; revised, the story was accepted by *The New Yorker*.

59

"Ex-Basketball Player with Gasoline Station"

Flick once played for the high school team, the Demons.

Two pages from early drafts and *New Yorker* printer's copy of the poem; Moretown, Vt., [n.d.]. bMS Am 1793.1 (9) and (25).

60

"By Himself"

Although he was not really a brutal young man . . .

. . . He walked faster, almost running, running.

First and last words of an early story about an unnamed young man on the day his wife enters the maternity hospital; annotated "*no good*" and never submitted for publication. TS. with A.MS. revisions and annotations; [n.p., n.d.]. *86M-3 (30)

61

Rabbit, Run

A few A.MS. and TS. notes for early drafts and revisions in successive editions; includes fragments of text and rejected pages selected from 329 sheets of such notes in bMS Am 1793.7 (169)

Rabbit, Run
present tense
a motion picture

Rabbit, Run
enter: basketball; kids playing; scramble of legs, etc., while the credits run

expand Tothero part   *expand car ride— more, more*

Remembered love is beautiful,
present love is lifelike,
imagined love is obscene

. . . domestic idyll; go to church; lust aroused; deserts; drown baby

BABY in tub [with drawing]

her soliloquy

. . . whore or wife

Crocuses break the crust . . .

Soggy (Rabbit thus caps his summary of Eccles)

"I ran all the way home / Just to say I'm sorry"

R. thinks— there was once something excellent, . . .

his insistence on some deep rightness in his random,
and disastrous, actions.

; mindlessly, runs

. . . he runs. Runs.

Ah: runs, Runs.

62

Rabbit, Run

In Rabbit: *show Eccles' mood of deflation and fatigue after Harry comes back.*

Note for the novel written on the first draft of the short story "The Sea's Green Monotony" / "The Sea's Green Sameness"; [Antigua? Mar 1960].
bMS Am 1793.1 (25) item 33

63

Rabbit, Run

Rabbit less good at golf because can't make club part of self

Notes for the novel on a page of the first draft of "Pigeon Feathers" (originally "Killing Pigeons"). A.MS.; [n.p., n.d.].
bMS Am 1793.1 (23) item 31

64

Rabbit, Run: A Motion Picture

. . . a little boy with slow reflexes . . .

Pages from draft of the novel, A.MS. and TS. with A.MS. revisions; [Ipswich, 1959]. In this version of the opening scene, seven— not six— boys are playing basketball around a telephone pole in an alley, while a smaller child watches. bMS Am 1793.7 (169).

65

Rabbit, Run

Everybody except the ~~*boy*~~ *slow kid laughs*

In this later draft, the child at the foot of the telephone pole is hit by Rabbit's first shot at the basket. TS. with A.MS. revisions; Ipswich, 1959–1960. bMS Am 1793.1 (170)

66

Rabbit, Run

Everybody except one slow kid laughs

Here it is one of the players, not the child himself, who doesn't laugh when the basketball hits the child. The change from "the" to "one" may have been the result of a misreading of Updike's handwritten revision in the manuscript from which both Knopf and Gollancz set galleys.

Galleys for a Victor Gollancz edition; London, 1960. With February 1960 memorandum of agreement between Updike and Victor Gollancz, Ltd.; London, 1960. bMS Am 1793.7 (177) and *80M-11 (1089)

67

Rabbit, Run

"Luck," one of the kids says.
"Skill," he answers, . . .

The child watching the game disappears in this version. Knopf's first galleys followed the manuscript; some changes were made later.

Galleys for the Knopf first edition with A.MS. and TS. revisions and MS. annotations in various hands; New York and Ipswich, Apr–Jun 1960. bMS Am 1793.7 (171)

68

Rabbit, Run: "Supplementary Sheet— new series no. 300."

Harry, or Rabbit, Angstrom was once a first-rate baseball player.

Victor Gollancz's advertisement, mimeographed with revisions by Gollancz; London, 1960. bMS Am 1793.7 (178)

69

Rabbit, Run: "Author's Note to English Edition"

Those passages in the American text of this novel which my English publishers have felt unable to print . . .

The writing of fiction is not a form of social intercourse in which good manners obtain . . .

TS. draft with A.MS. revisions of note dated May 1960 which was to have accompanied a Gollancz edition; Ipswich, 1960. bMS Am 1793.7 (176)

Gollancz had made some changes in the text, particularly in the scenes with Ruth, before galleys were composed, and he proposed other changes. It was Andre Deutsch who brought out the first English edition the following year.

70

Rabbit, Run

He calculates, A dime a pound.

Uncut page proofs for Knopf first edition, with A.MS. and TS. revisions and MS. annotations in various hands; New York and Ipswich, Jun 1960. bMS Am 1793.7 (173)

71

Rabbit, Run

O.K. to lock

Uncut page proofs for Knopf first edition with MS. annotations in various hands; New York, Aug 1960. bMS Am 1793.7 (174)

72

Rabbit, Run

Sitting there by himself he comes to the conclusion that either he or his mother must die.

Copy of the Deutsch 1961 edition with MS. annotations (Anglicizing spelling) and revisions, and A.MS. and TS. revisions for the 1964 Penguin edition. London and Ipswich; 1964. *68-430

Some of the additions to the text of the Penguin edition come from previously unprinted passages in the draft.

73

The Poorhouse Fair *Rabbit, Run:* "Foreword"

. . . I felt impelled to rework all proofs heavily and, after the book was published, to make further revisions for the Penguin edition . . .

Printer's copy of the Foreword to the 1965 Modern Library collection of the two novels. TS. with A.MS. revisions and MS. annotations; Ipswich, 1964. With sheets of the Penguin paperback marked for the Modern Library edition. *68-429

74

Rabbit, Run

He seems to leave behind him in the cafeteria . . .

Galley proofs with A.MS., TS. and print (cut pages of Deutsch edition) revisions and MS. annotations in various hands for the 1970 Knopf revised fifth edition, now in print; New York and Ipswich, 1969. With mounted tear sheets for this edition including A.MS. and MS. annotations and revisions. A later Knopf printing mistakenly reprinted the earlier unrevised text. *70M-24

Design: Greer Allen
Typesetting: Custom Printing and Typographic Service
Printing: Meriden-Stinehour Press
Binding: Mueller Trade Bindery

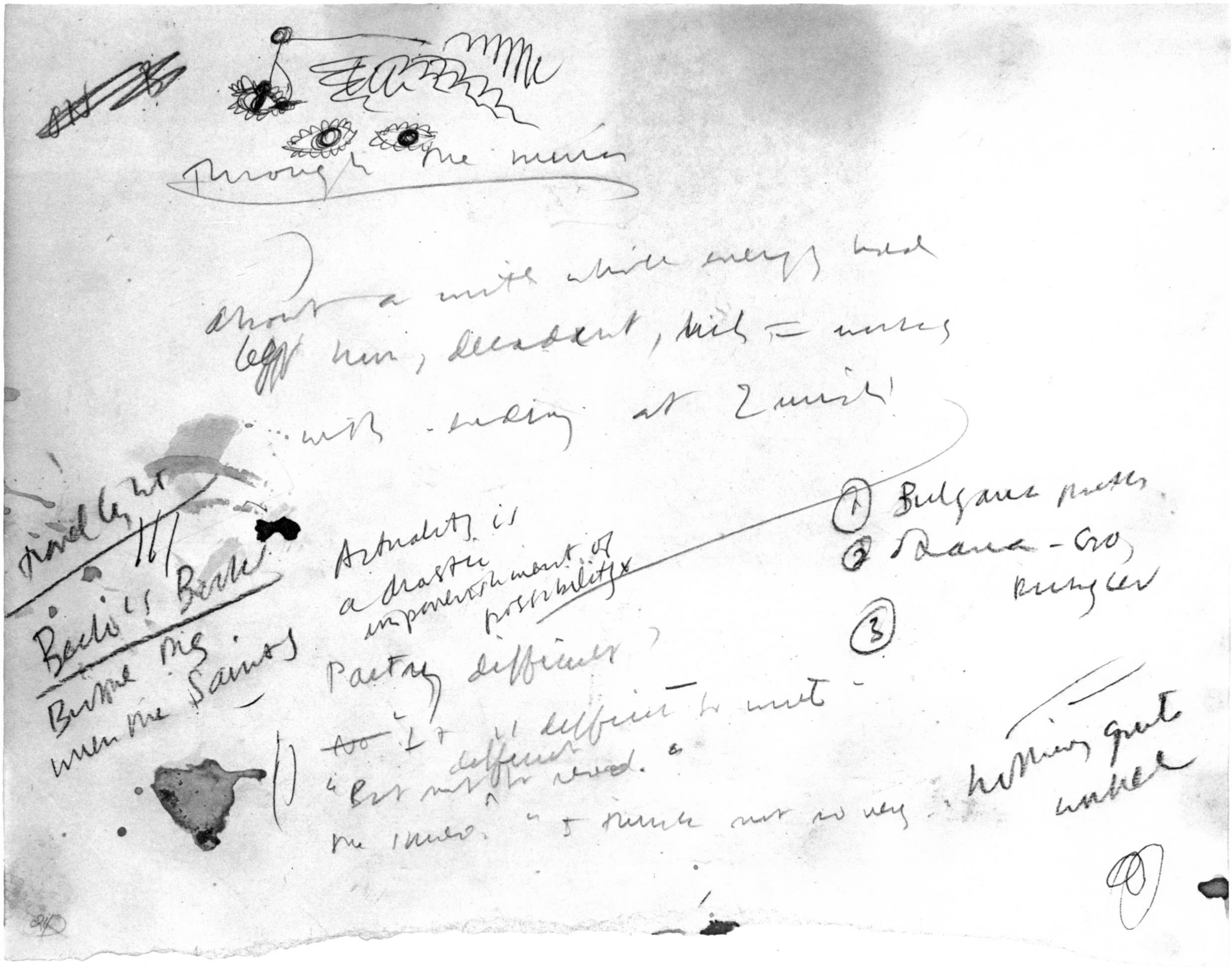

1. Early notes for "The Bulgarian Poetess," here titled "Through the Mirror."

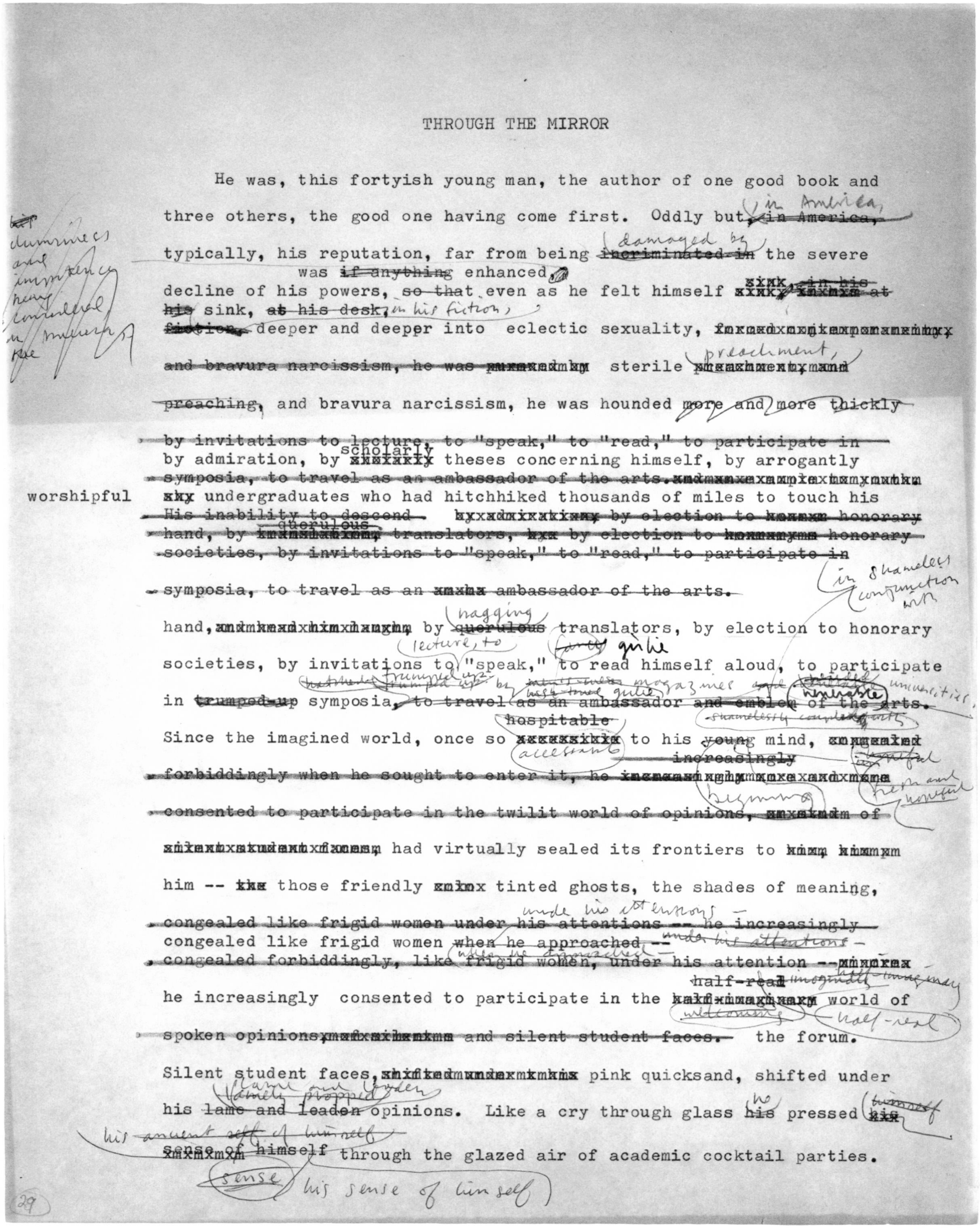

THROUGH THE MIRROR

He was, this fortyish young man, the author of one good book and three others, the good one having come first. Oddly but, in America, typically, his reputation, far from being incriminated in the severe decline of his powers, was if anything enhanced, so that even as he felt himself sink, at his desk, deeper and deeper into eclectic sexuality, sterile preachment, and bravura narcissism, he was hounded more and more thickly by admiration, by scholarly theses concerning himself, by arrogantly worshipful undergraduates who had hitchhiked thousands of miles to touch his hand, by nagging translators, by election to honorary societies, by invitations to "speak," to read himself aloud, to participate in trumped-up symposia, to travel as an ambassador and emblem of the arts. Since the imagined world, once so hospitable to his young mind, increasingly had virtually sealed its frontiers to him -- those friendly tinted ghosts, the shades of meaning, congealed like frigid women when he approached -- he increasingly consented to participate in the half-real world of the forum. Silent student faces, pink quicksand, shifted under his lame and leaden opinions. Like a cry through glass his pressed sense of himself through the glazed air of academic cocktail parties.

1. First page of first draft of "The Bulgarian Poetess," introducing Henry Bech.

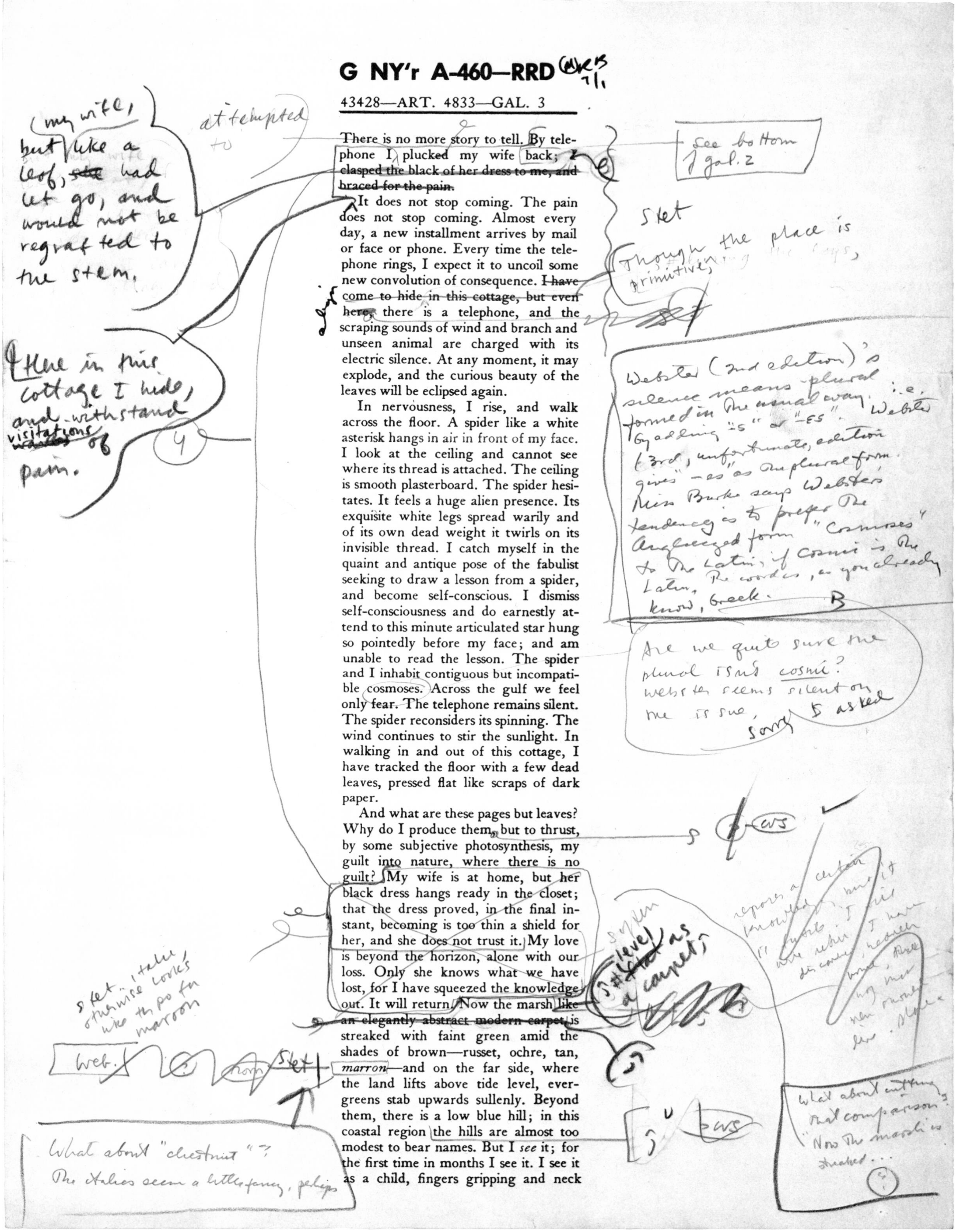

G NY'r A-460—RRD

43428—ART. 4833—GAL. 3

There is no more story to tell. By telephone I plucked my wife back; I clasped the black of her dress to me, and braced for the pain.

It does not stop coming. The pain does not stop coming. Almost every day, a new installment arrives by mail or face or phone. Every time the telephone rings, I expect it to uncoil some new convolution of consequence. I have come to hide in this cottage, but even here, there is a telephone, and the scraping sounds of wind and branch and unseen animal are charged with its electric silence. At any moment, it may explode, and the curious beauty of the leaves will be eclipsed again.

In nervousness, I rise, and walk across the floor. A spider like a white asterisk hangs in air in front of my face. I look at the ceiling and cannot see where its thread is attached. The ceiling is smooth plasterboard. The spider hesitates. It feels a huge alien presence. Its exquisite white legs spread warily and of its own dead weight it twirls on its invisible thread. I catch myself in the quaint and antique pose of the fabulist seeking to draw a lesson from a spider, and become self-conscious. I dismiss self-consciousness and do earnestly attend to this minute articulated star hung so pointedly before my face; and am unable to read the lesson. The spider and I inhabit contiguous but incompatible cosmoses. Across the gulf we feel only fear. The telephone remains silent. The spider reconsiders its spinning. The wind continues to stir the sunlight. In walking in and out of this cottage, I have tracked the floor with a few dead leaves, pressed flat like scraps of dark paper.

And what are these pages but leaves? Why do I produce them, but to thrust, by some subjective photosynthesis, my guilt into nature, where there is no guilt? My wife is at home, but her black dress hangs ready in the closet; that the dress proved, in the final instant, becoming is too thin a shield for her, and she does not trust it. My love is beyond the horizon, alone with our loss. Only she knows what we have lost, for I have squeezed the knowledge out. It will return. Now the marsh like an elegantly abstract modern carpet is streaked with faint green amid the shades of brown—russet, ochre, tan, marron—and on the far side, where the land lifts above tide level, evergreens stab upwards sullenly. Beyond them, there is a low blue hill; in this coastal region the hills are almost too modest to bear names. But I *see* it; for the first time in months I see it. I see it as a child, fingers gripping and neck

5. *New Yorker* galley of "Leaves," showing author's dialogue with editor William Maxwell ("B") and printers' marks.

12

anonymous, the end of his quest for fame. Pascal says, We love writers because they disclose to (us) ~~ourselves~~ ~~the~~ riches that are our own.

Beginning, then, with cunning private ambitions and (a) rather (piquant) ~~narrow~~ fascination with the implements of graphic representation, I find myself arrived, in this (audible search ~~before you~~) for self-justification, at a (curious) (embarassed) ~~hope of~~ altruism, ~~a generous, if not grandiose, conception of the writer's worth.~~ Beginning with the wish to make an impression, (one ends) ~~he must say~~ (wishing to erase the impression, to make of it a perfect) ~~something, and that something can only be his life, his life~~ (transparency, to make of oneself a point ~~whereby the world~~) ~~with its full penumbra of observation and thought, and he ends by offering his~~ (of focus purely, as) ~~life as of value only in that it~~ (is) ~~been a transparency, a lens looking into other lives.~~ (selfless as a lens. ~~From love of one goes from a ...~~) ~~The writer of fiction of poetry begins with~~ (~~little tyrant's delight ... in wielding a pencil to a~~) ~~personal truth, but~~ does not end (~~middle-aged a~~) ~~there; a curious communion widens out from those first published accounts of the mysterious life we led before we became writers and, that first wave of self-expression exhausted, we wait, as the ocean between waves waits, for another surge to arrive, less dense than the first it may be, thinner but more generous and ideal, irradiated with borrowed light, yet still, as waves are, playful and transcendent.~~ (one begins by seeking attention and)

~~one must say something, and that something can only be our life,~~
~~to erase it, to wish~~
one ends by ~~wishing oneself away, by~~ feeling a terrible impatience with everything -- every flattering attention, every invitation to speak and to impersonate a wise man, ~~or celebrity~~, every hunger of the ego and of the body -- an impatience with everything that clouds and clots (our) ~~us~~, (ecstatic witness to the world ~~that is~~ that) ~~one~~ ~~that delays the perfect moment when becomes merely a point where two worlds impinge, the world as it has been given to us to know it, and the other enormity, the silent mind of the reader.~~ (surrounds and transcends us. A writer begins with his personal truth, with that obscure but ~~intense and~~)

7. Draft of "Why Write?" s. 12, including various A.MS. and TS. revisions.

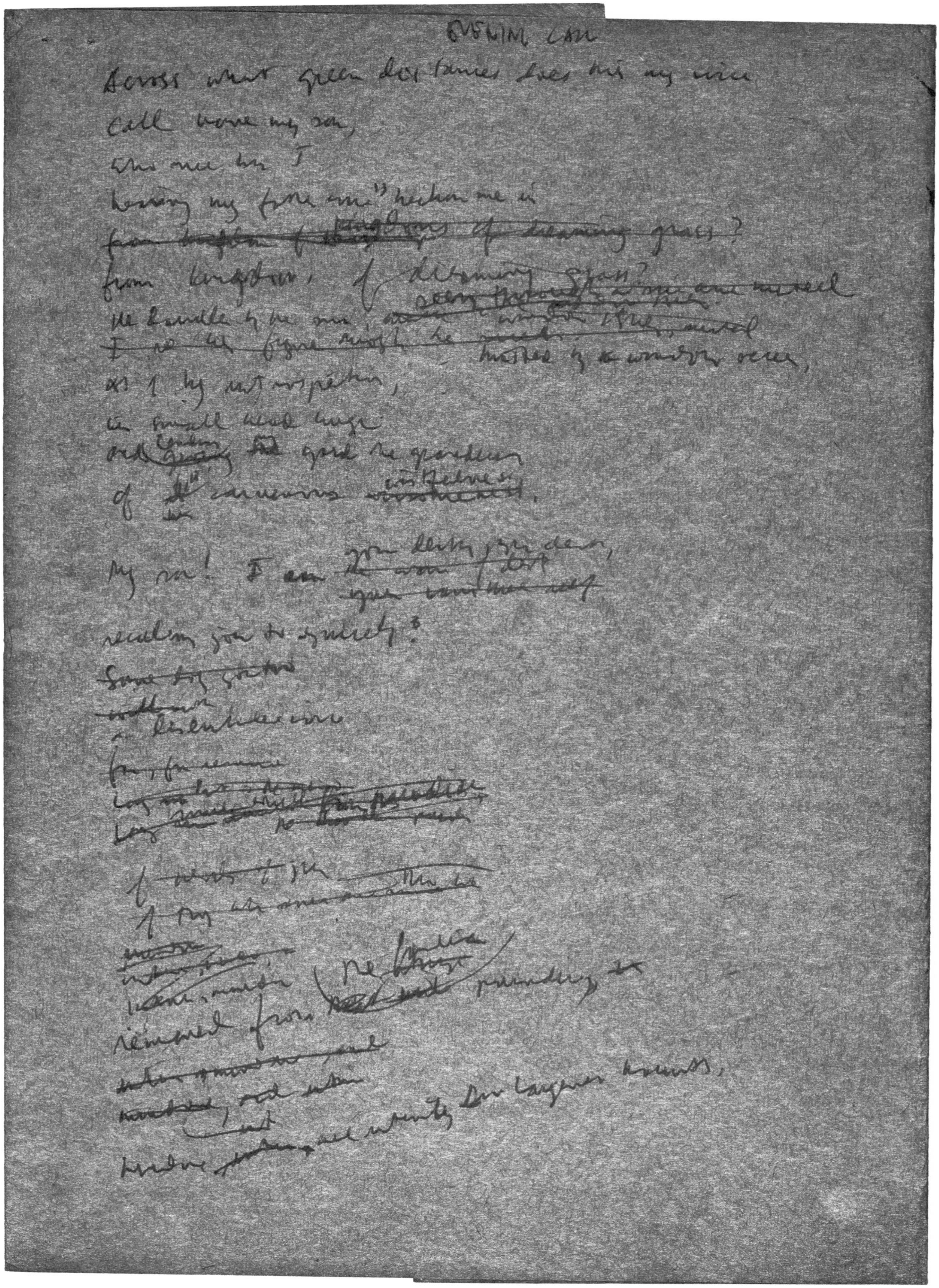
Across what green distances does my voice
call home my son,
who once was I

8. Beginning of first draft of "Call," written on a *New York Review of Books* mailing envelope.

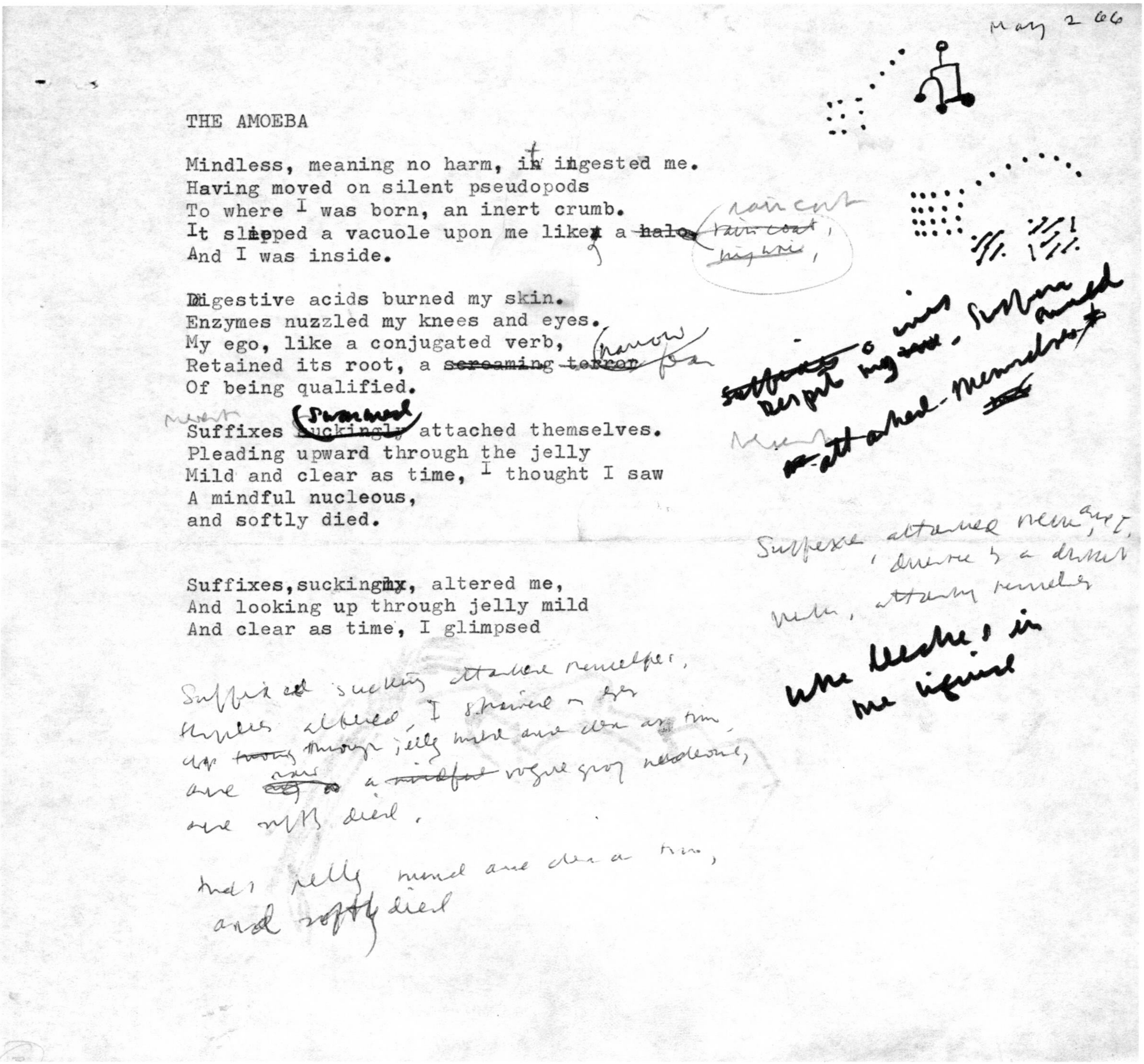

May 2 66

THE AMOEBA

Mindless, meaning no harm, it ingested me.
Having moved on silent pseudopods
To where I was born, an inert crumb.
It slipped a vacuole upon me like a ~~halo~~ rain coat,
And I was inside.

Digestive acids burned my skin.
Enzymes nuzzled my knees and eyes.
My ego, like a conjugated verb,
Retained its root, a ~~screaming terror~~ narrow fear
Of being qualified.

Suffixes ~~suckingly~~ attached themselves.
Pleading upward through the jelly
Mild and clear as time, I thought I saw
A mindful nucleous,
and softly died.

Suffixes, suckingly, altered me,
And looking up through jelly mild
And clear as time, I glimpsed

and softly died

10. Early TS. draft of "The Amoeba" with A.MS. revisions including variations of stanza 3.

Suffixes, sucking, swarmed.
I lost my mother's arms, my teeth,
my laugh, my memories, my faith.

Alas, suffixes swarmed.
I lost my mother's arms, my teeth,
my laugh, my protruding faith.
Reduced to the O of a final sigh,
obediently I died.

Alas, suffixed swarmed.
I lost my mother's arms, my teeth,
my laugh, my protruding faith.
Reduced to the O of a final sigh,
in time I died.

Alas, suffixes swarmed.

Suffixes, cu

Suffi a

Suffixes, swarming, die

Suffixes, sucking, swarmed.
I lost my mother's arms, my teeth,
my laugh, my protruding faith.
Reduced to the O of a sigh,
in time I died.

Alas, suffixes swarmed.
I lost my mother's arms, my teeth,
my laugh, my protruding faith.
Reduced to theO

Suffixes war

Suffixes swarmed.

Alas, suffixes swarmed.

Suffixes swarmed.

I lost my arms, my laugh,

Suffixes swarmed.
I lost my arms, my laugh,
my memories, my protruding faith.
Transparent as time, I joined ~~xxx~~ the jelly,
And softly died.

Suffixes, sucking, swarmed.
I lost my mother's arms,
my laugh, my protruding faith.
Upward through jelly I cried,
and softly died.

Suffixes, sucking, swarmed.
I lost my mother's arms,
my laugh, my protruding faith.
Reduced to the O of a sigh,

Suffixes, sucking, swarmed.
I lost my mother's arms, my teeth,
my laugh and protruding faith.
Reduced to the O of a sigh,
I softly died.

10. Pieces of two sheets with additional variations of "The Amoeba," stanza 3.

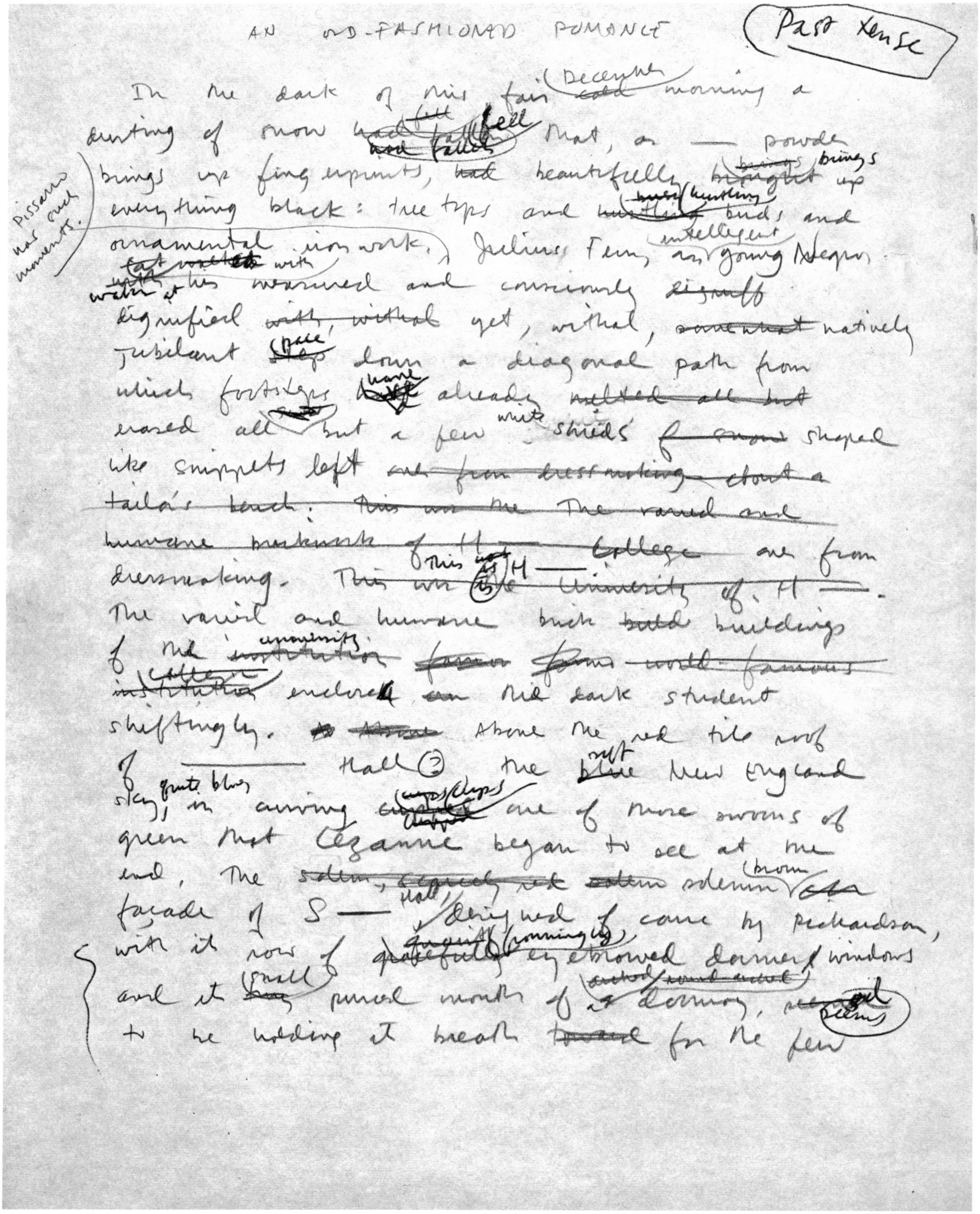

AN OLD-FASHIONED ROMANCE

Past tense

In the dark of this fair December morning a bunting of snow fell that, as — powder brings up fingerprints, beautifully brings up everything black: tree tops and bristling buds and ornamental ironwork. Julius Fenn, an intelligent young Negro, with his wearied and consciously dignified yet, withal, natively jubilant pace down a diagonal path from which footsteps have already erased all but a few white shreds shaped like snippets left from dressmaking. This is H— University. The varied and humane brick buildings of the university enclosed the dark student shiftingly. Above the red tile roof of ___ Hall (?) the soft New England sky, quite blue, in curving slips one of those swoons of green that Cézanne began to see at the end, the solemn brown facade of S— Hall, designed of course by Richardson, with its row of winning eyebrowed dormer windows and its small punial mouth of a doorway, seems to be holding its breath for the few

Pissarro has such moments.

13. One of eight versions of the beginning of an unfinished novel, here titled *An Old-Fashioned Romance*.

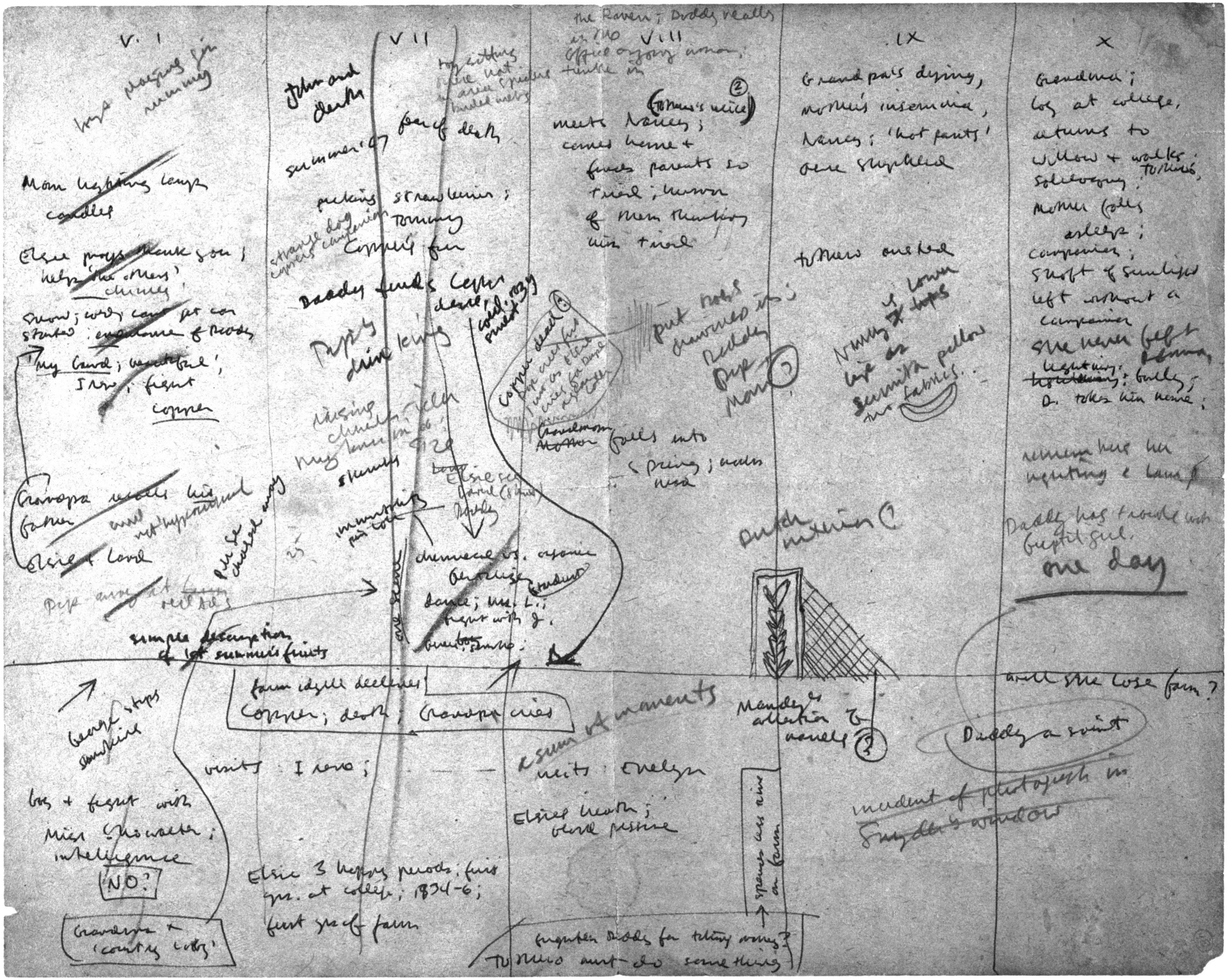

14. Page of plot diagram for chapters VI–X of *Home*, an unpublished novel.

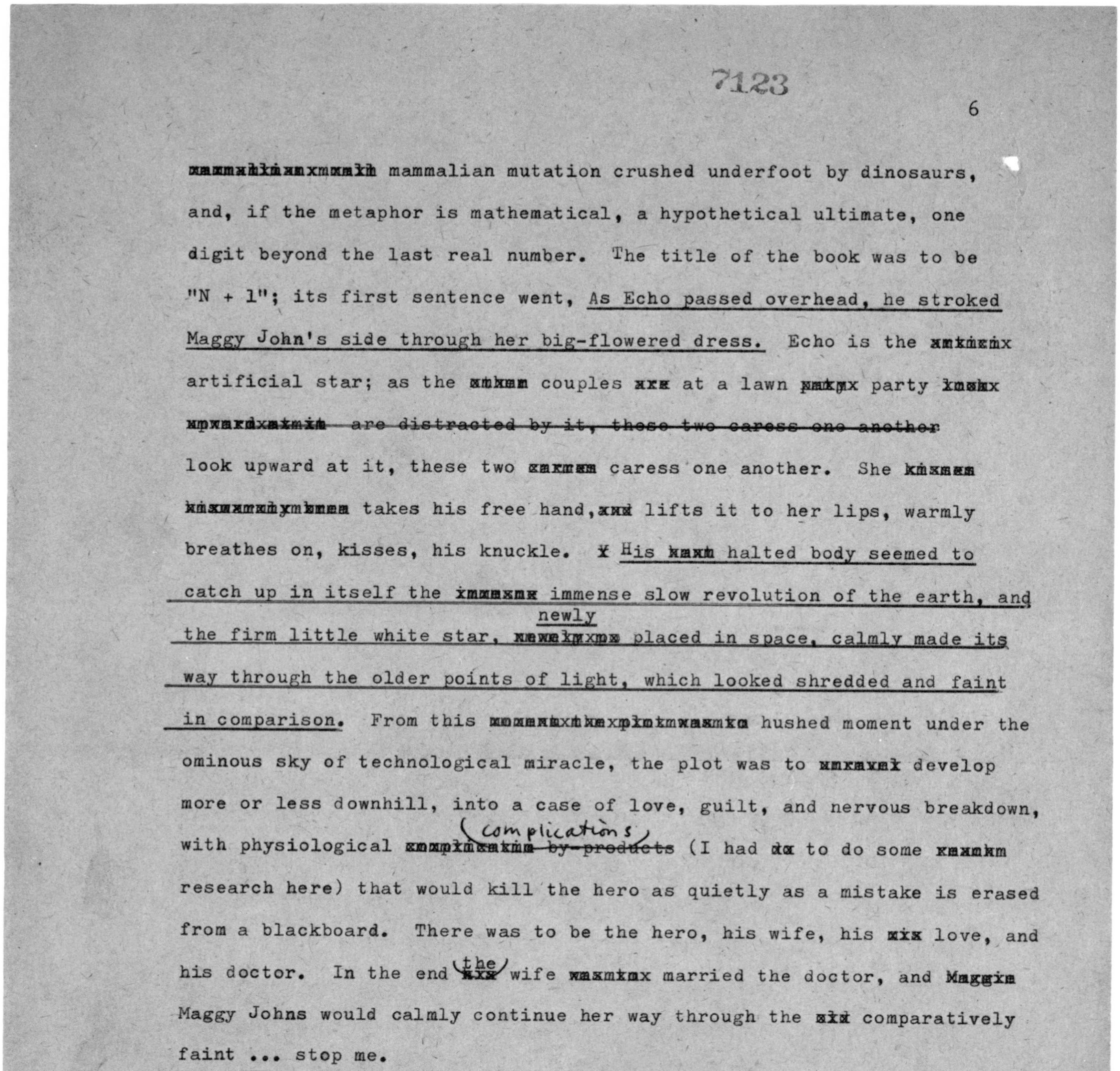

7123

6

~~xxxxxxxxxxxxxx~~ mammalian mutation crushed underfoot by dinosaurs, and, if the metaphor is mathematical, a hypothetical ultimate, one digit beyond the last real number. The title of the book was to be "N + 1"; its first sentence went, As Echo passed overhead, he stroked Maggy John's side through her big-flowered dress. Echo is the ~~xxxxxx~~ artificial star; as the ~~xxxxx~~ couples ~~xxx~~ at a lawn ~~xxxxx~~ party ~~xxxxx xxxxxxxxxxx~~ ~~are distracted by it, these two caress one another~~ look upward at it, these two ~~xxxxx~~ caress one another. She ~~xxxxxx xxxxxxxxxxxx~~ takes his free hand, ~~xxx~~ lifts it to her lips, warmly breathes on, kisses, his knuckle. ~~x~~ His ~~xxxx~~ halted body seemed to catch up in itself the ~~xxxxxxx~~ immense slow revolution of the earth, and the firm little white star, newly ~~xxxxxxxxx~~ placed in space, calmly made its way through the older points of light, which looked shredded and faint in comparison. From this ~~xxxxxxxxxxxxxxxxxxxxx~~ hushed moment under the ominous sky of technological miracle, the plot was to ~~xxxxxxx~~ develop more or less downhill, into a case of love, guilt, and nervous breakdown, with physiological complications ~~xxxxxxxxxx by-products~~ (I had ~~xx~~ to do some ~~xxxxxx~~ research here) that would kill the hero as quietly as a mistake is erased from a blackboard. There was to be the hero, his wife, his ~~xxx~~ love, and his doctor. In the end the ~~xxx~~ wife ~~xxxxxxx~~ married the doctor, and ~~xxxxxx~~ Maggy Johns would calmly continue her way through the ~~xxx~~ comparatively faint ... stop me.

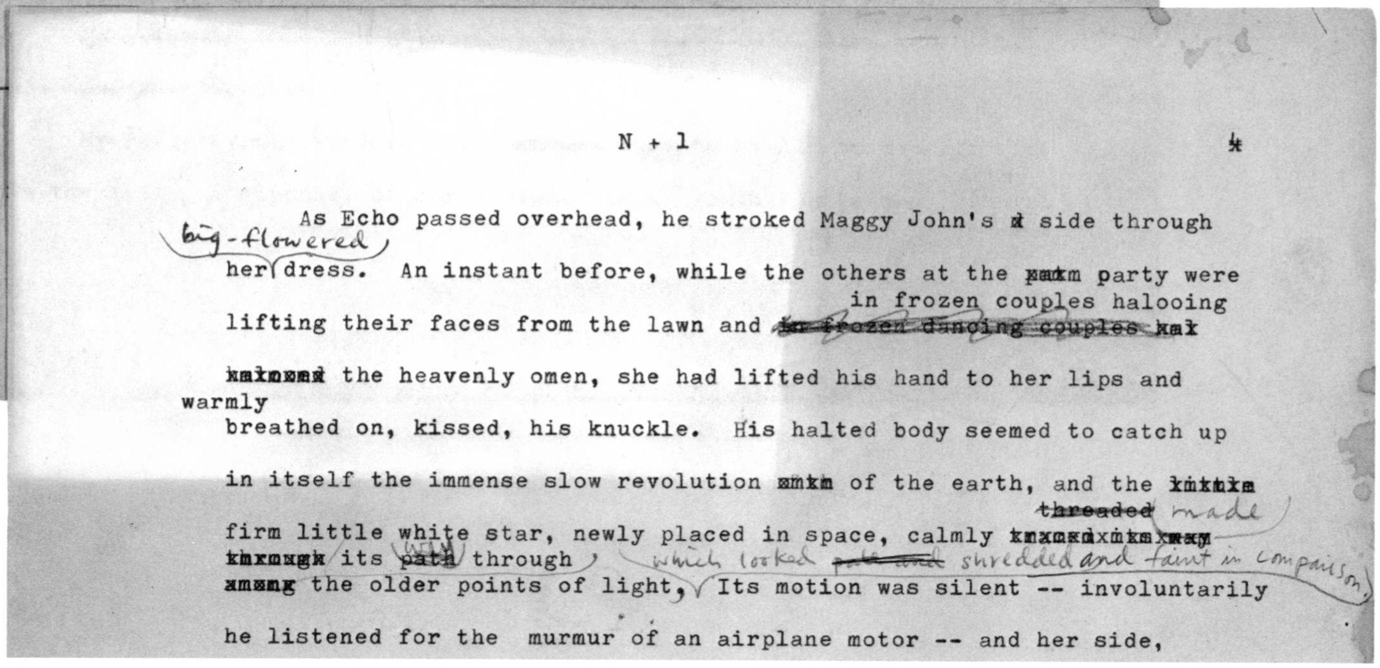

N + 1

4

As Echo passed overhead, he stroked Maggy John's ~~x~~ side through her big-flowered dress. An instant before, while the others at the ~~xxxx~~ party were lifting their faces from the lawn and in frozen couples halooing ~~in frozen dancing couples xxx xxxxxx~~ the heavenly omen, she had lifted his hand to her lips and warmly breathed on, kissed, his knuckle. His halted body seemed to catch up in itself the immense slow revolution ~~xxxx~~ of the earth, and the ~~xxxxxx~~ firm little white star, newly placed in space, calmly ~~threaded~~ made ~~xxxxxxxxxxxxx xxxxxxx~~ its ~~path~~ way through ~~xxxxx~~ the older points of light, which looked ~~pale and~~ shredded and faint in comparison. Its motion was silent -- involuntarily he listened for the murmur of an airplane motor -- and her side,

18 & 19. Passage from the story "The Music School" describing an unwritten novel, with passage from *N + 1*.

I look around for my girls, but they're gone, of course. There~~'s nobody~~ wasn't anybody but some young married screaming with her children about some candy they didn't get by the door of a blue Falcon station wagon. Looking back in the big windows, over the bags of peat moss and aluminum furniture stacked on the pavement, I ~~can~~ could see Lengel in my place in the slot, checking the sheep through. His face ~~is~~ was dark gray and his back stiff, as if he'd just had an injection of iron, and my stomach kind of ~~falls as~~ fell I ~~realize~~ felt how hard the world~~'s~~ was going to be to me ~~hereafter~~ thereafter.

/m JOHN UPDIKE — 11-pt etsc flush right

LET me tell you about the beach. The old people are usually there by the time I get down. They come down early because they have nothing to do but have forgotten how to sleep. Dressed in funny old suits, with oval tops and frilly skirts, the ladies walk back and forth in straw hats, back and forth, picking up shells and smiling at the seagulls. There's an old gent, with a bald head and a brown barrel chest with white hair all over it, who wears a very skimpy tight kind of French-style

With what timidity, with what a sense of trespass, do I set forward even this obliquely a thought so official! Forgive me. I am not yet ordained; I am too disordered to deal with the main text. My competence is marginal, and I will confine myself to the gloss of flesh with which this particular margin, this one beach, is annotated each day.

Here the cinema of life is run backwards. The old are the first to arrive. They ~~have lost the blessings of occupation and~~ are idle, and have lost the gift of sleep. Each of our bodies is a clock that loses time. Young as I am, I can hear in myself the protein acids ticking; I have observed how the older we get, the fewer the mornings left to us, the hungrier we become for daylight. The old ladies wear wide straw hats and in their hats'

20 & 21. Passage from the story "A & P" showing where the original story was cut, with passage from the new story "Lifeguard" made from the discarded text.

story -- You Vulptuous Piece of Wallpaper, You
Like the Jack of Hearts, A had only one eye. Milky center, never noticed except when some image like, across room to J., look like a piece of wallpaper. What happens? Jack -- inspirer, stirrer -- of hearts.

Like the Jack of Hearts, Nelson Morrison had only one eye. ~~(in childhood to his brother's BB gun and his mother's Christian Science.~~ faith healing
He had lost the left ~~to a BB in a childhood.~~ Now an athletic and xathanxmxheavily rather heavily ahantnanim ahumdily handsome xairplanexpartsxsalesmanxengineman salesman of airplane partsx, ~~thirty years old exactly, he carried~~ he lay on the Xaddinxghanks Weddingtons' ~~plush~~ (Esterbagh grass colored green) sofa as if in the cooling shade of his ~~thirty~~ 29 years, and no one felt sorry for him. Many at the party didn't even know of his the handicap -- which fug figured with such prominence xx him humiliatingly in his driver's license, his job applications, his his 4-F card -- and imaginedpthendeadxeyexhooked, if they imagined at all, that his eyes watered mmxmum because he drank too much. Even Richard, when Nelson suddenly called through the smoke in hisx his loud but ~~xxxxxx~~ shy ~~apologetic~~ (usually tactful) amxhum voice to Mary Brewer, "Mary, to me you're sitting there in that red chair like a xmkp voluptuous piece of wallpaper," didn't kmmmmfmm for some seconds realize kxmwxwhat the was xmmmxm source of ~~his~~ sense of justness, of a xf x kmmnikmff beautiful ~~truth~~ (brilliance justness fittingness) in things so ~~sharp~~ that tears absurdly stung his own eyes.

Mary, who had been dreaming, xiththingxthemm xx xxpmsed in repose in the red chair in a largely patterned print dress that like all her

and discover that the xxxx shed is xmxflant on our right not our left, then that there are two pearxthm pear xpple trees instead of one, and that the pxixx box hedge is lower than we remembered.

~~My love xkxx expandam advanced slowly expanded slowly, released by random accidents. At xmparky another party, Nix Morris~~

There ixxmm was no sense of dawn in my love. Each advance she made into me, or I into her, was conquest of territory already, ~~in~~ somehow, ~~mysterious way, already~~ mapped. The signposts seemed planted before we came to them. Nix Morris, (whom alcohol turned metaphoric,) ~~who became lyrical when drunk, once called across a room to her while she sat in a chair dress where she sat dressed imxmax while she sat who became metaphoric when drunk,~~ once loudly called across a room to her that she looked "like a voluptuous piece of wmxhpapex wallpaper." She was wearing a print dress patterned with big orange flowers. She blushed, and a ~~kind of~~ jealous panic tore at my heart, that others could see

22, 22, 23. Note and section from one draft of "You Voluptuous Piece of Wallpaper, You," with passage from "Couples."

styles, were for me like the mental adjustments made when, after many years, we return to a childhood scene and discover that the shed is on our right and not our left, that there are two pear trees instead of one, and that the box hedge ~~is lower~~ (extends further) than we remembered.

In our (small) society, where the woman tended to dress quietly in the simple facts of their names, assets, and educations, Peggy's clothes were ~~slightly~~ ~~rather~~ (a bit) spectacular. Nix Morris, whom alcohol turned metaphorical, once loudly called across a room to her that she looked "like a voluptuous piece of wallpaper." She was wearing a silk sheath dress patterned with big orange flowers. She blushed, ~~blushed like a pioneer~~.

like the mental adjustments made when, after many years, we return to a childhood scene and discover that the shed is on our right and not our left, that there are two pears trees instead of one, and that the box hedge is lower than we remembered.

In our conservative society, where the woman dress quietly in their names, their backgrounds, and their educations, ~~ancestry, and their education,~~ her clothes were rather spectacular. It was xlmoxt as if she brought with her from the Midwest xmmmk something of the Indian and of calico. Nix Morrismmxwhomxalcoholxturnxdm Morris, ~~inxwhomxalcohol whom alcohol released into unknown dimensions of metaphor~~ inxwhom in whom alcohol released streams of metaphor that the brokerage business bottled, once loudly calledacross a room to her that she looked likex like "a voluptuous piece of wallpaper." She was sitting in the Woodworth's wing chair and wearing a print sheath dress -- could it have been silk? -- patterned with big orange flowers. Xxklxm

Those summer parties. ~~Why can't I remember?~~ (Should remember them better.) Female shoulders crossed by cotton straps. Sunlight in the gin, the sprig of mint (wilting). The smell of grass freshly mowed coming in through the evening screens. Children coming in and out with come xxx complaint that xxxx time more than the mother soothed.

Katharine's husband Jerry had one eye, the other frosted by a xhixkxm childhood accident. No one felt sorry for him, he was so hearty. (A born salesman.) Him saying across to Sarah Harris, her pregnant in a big-flowered dress, "Sarah you look ~~just~~ like a voluptuous big piece of wallpaper ~~sitting there!~~" I thought, Has only one eye, everything looks flat to him. Sickening sensation of love, for everyone there. Xxxxxxxxxxxxx

24, 24, 26. Sections from drafts of "Peggy's Clothes," "Judith's Clothes," and "When Everyone Was Pregnant."

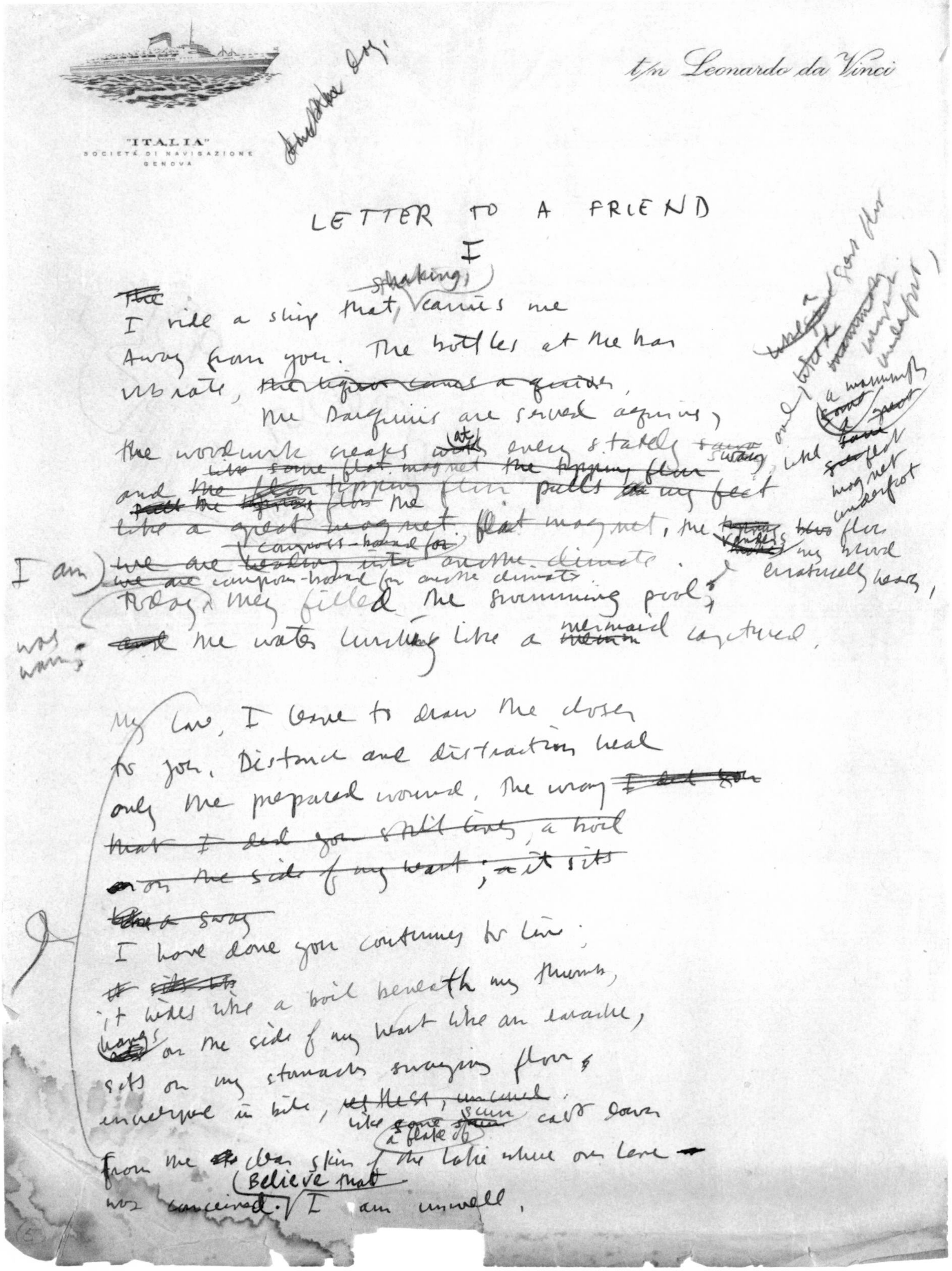
"ITALIA"
SOCIETÀ DI NAVIGAZIONE
GENOVA

t/n Leonardo da Vinci

LETTER TO A FRIEND

I

~~The~~
I ride a ship that, shaking, carries me
Away from you. The bottles at the bar
vibrate, ~~the liquor ... a quiver,~~
the daiquiris are served again,
the woodwork creaks at every stately ~~...~~ sway, like
~~like some flat magnet the tipping floor~~
and ~~the floor~~ tipping floor pulls ~~at~~ my feet
~~pull the tipping floor the~~
~~like a great magnet,~~ flat magnet, the ~~...~~ floor
~~we are heading into another climate.~~
I am) ~~we are~~ compass-bound for another climate.
Today, they filled the swimming pool,
was warm; ~~and~~ the water lurching like a mermaid captured.

My Love, I leave to draw the closer
to you. Distance and distraction heal
only the prepared wound. The wrong ~~I did you~~
~~that I did you still lasts~~, a boil
~~on the side of my heart~~; ~~it~~ sits
~~like a sway~~
I have done you continues to live;
~~it sits~~
it sits like a boil beneath my thumb,
hangs on the side of my heart like an earache,
sits on my stomach's swaying floor,
encased in bile, ~~...~~ like ~~some~~ a flake of scum cast down
from the clear skin of the lake where our love
was ~~conceived~~. Believe that I am unwell.

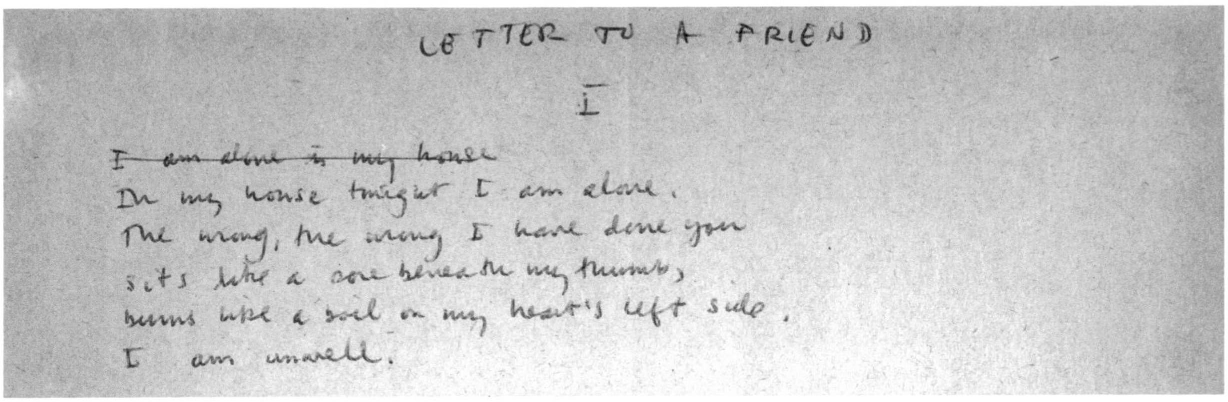
LETTER TO A FRIEND

I

~~I am alone in my house~~
In my house tonight I am alone.
The wrong, the wrong I have done you
sits like a sore beneath my thumb,
burns like a boil on my heart's left side.
I am unwell.

27. Page of first draft of the poem "Letter to a Friend," with fragment from a draft of "Report of Health" (here titled "Letter to a Friend.")

John Updike
c/o American Express
Cannes, France

TRISTAN

I ride a ship that, shaking, carries me
Away from you. The bottles at the bar
Vibrate, the Daiquiris are served aquiver,
The woodwork creaks ~~at~~ with every stately sway,
And, like a great flat magnet underfoot,
The floor renders my blood erratically heavy.
I am compass-bound for another climate.
Today was warm. They filled the swimming-pool,
The water lurching like a mermaid captured.

Of course I leave to draw the closer to you.
I feel your touch on every burnished latch;
A serviette, unfolded, yields your sigh.
Your memory's at home in luxury:
Pale-tesselated lavatories, foam,
White ropes, and dancing on a tipping floor.

Forgive me, I seem to be on a boat. The shock of leaving you numbed me rather nicely to the usual humiliations of boarding — why is it that everyone, no matter how well-born and self-confident, looks like a Central European immigrant in a pier shed, and is treated like one? — and even though we are now two days out to sea, and I can repose, ~~technically~~ technically, in your utter inaccessibility, I still am unable to focus on my fellow-passengers, though for a split-second of, ~~sanity I perceived that~~ as it were, absent-minded sanity, I did prophetically perceive, through a ~~flitting~~ chink in my obsession, that the waiter, having sized me up as one of the ~~ordinary~~ helpless solitaries of the world, would give me arrogant service and expect ~~at journey's end from me~~ ~~a~~ in turn, at journey's end, a ~~huge,~~ outsize, apologetic tip. He may be right. No matter. The next instant, I unfolded the napkin, and your ~~sigh~~ sigh, shaped exactly like a dove, the blue tint of its throat

I am sick~~x~~. The wrong I have done you is like a sore under my thumb, a crescent of bile ~~in my stomach~~ awash in my stomach. I am bleeding to death. Certainly I feel ~~bloodless~~ bloodless, or, more precisely, diluted, diluted by half, since everything around me — the white ropes, the ~~xxxxxxxxxxxxxx~~ lace ~~in our wake~~ of foam our prow tirelessly generates, ~~xxxxxxxxxx xxxxxxxxxxxxx~~ the really quite ingenious little catches that keep the doors from swinging, the charmingly tesselated ~~shower stall~~

27 & 28. Fragment of fair copy of the poem "Tristan," with two passages from a draft of the "Tristan" section of "Four Sides of One Story."

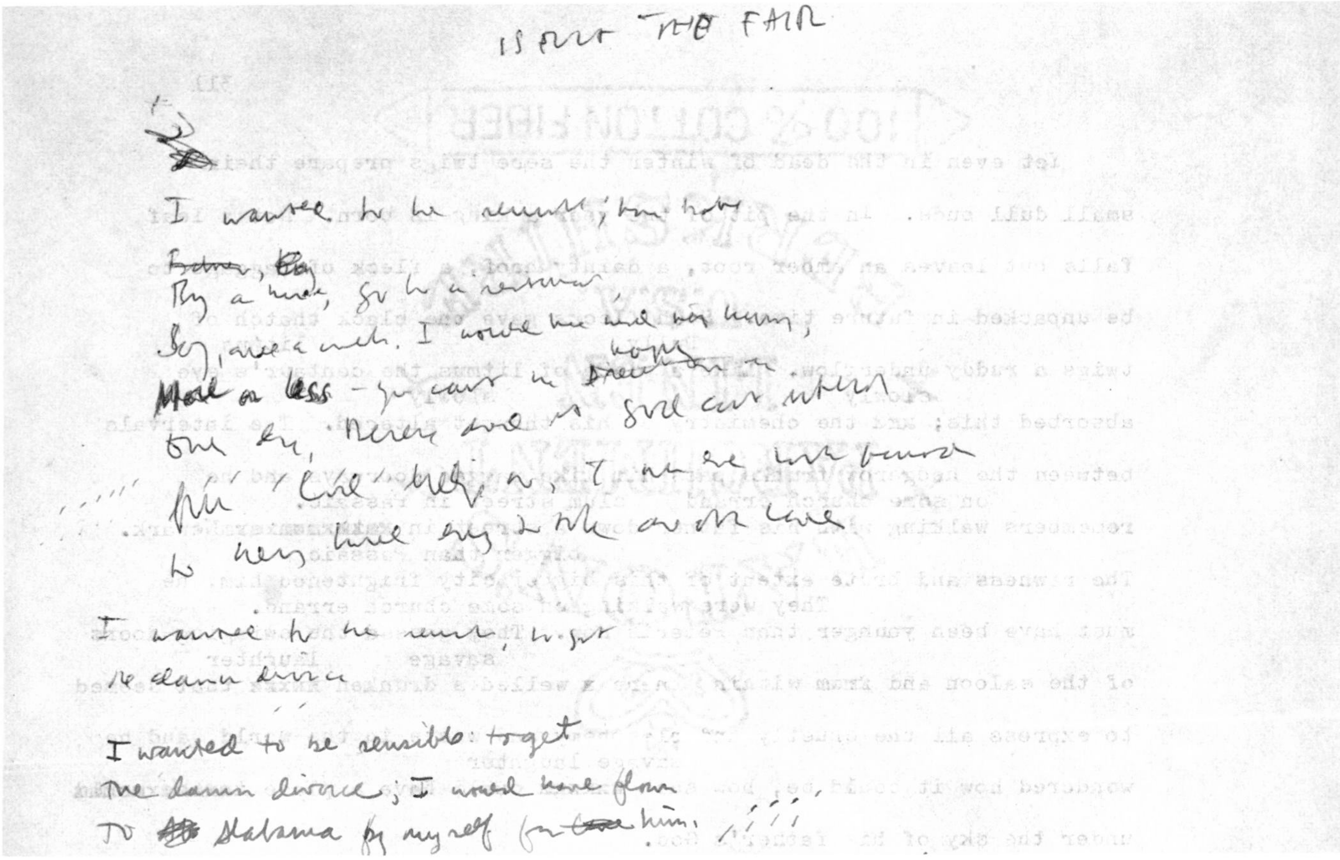
ISEULT THE FAIR
I wanted to be sensible: to get
the damn divorce, I would have flown
To Alabama by myself for him.

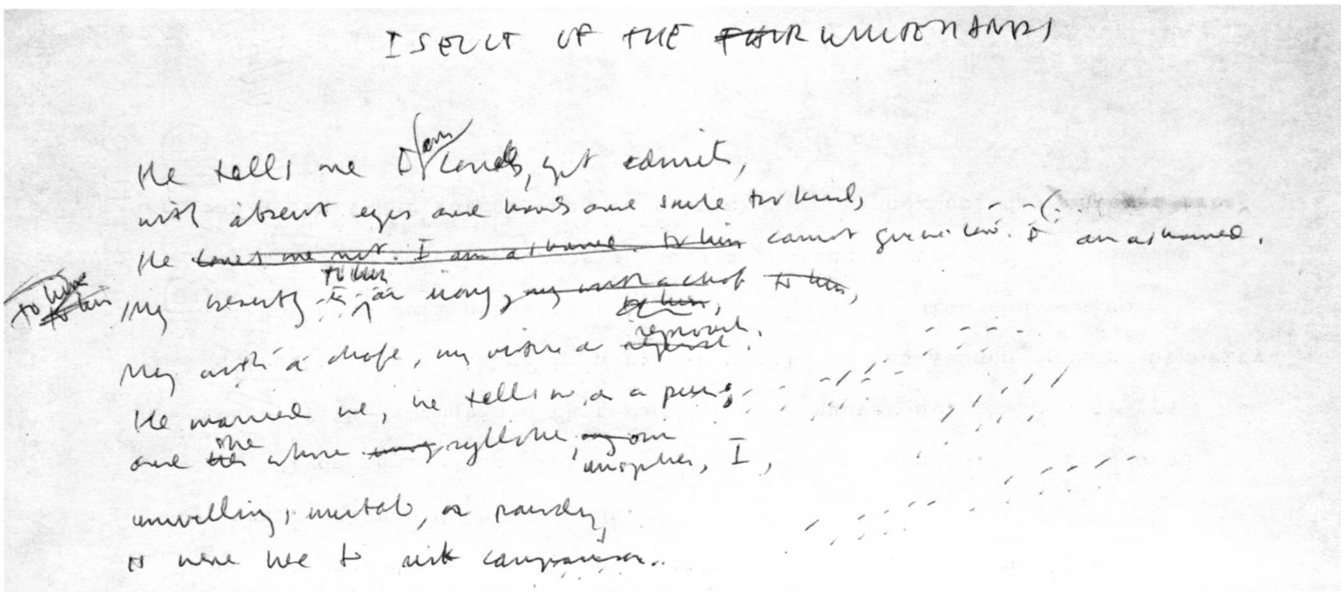
ISEULT OF THE ~~FAIR~~ WHITE HANDS
He tells me of his loneliness, yet admits,
with absent eyes and hands and smile too kind,
He married me, he tells me, on a passing

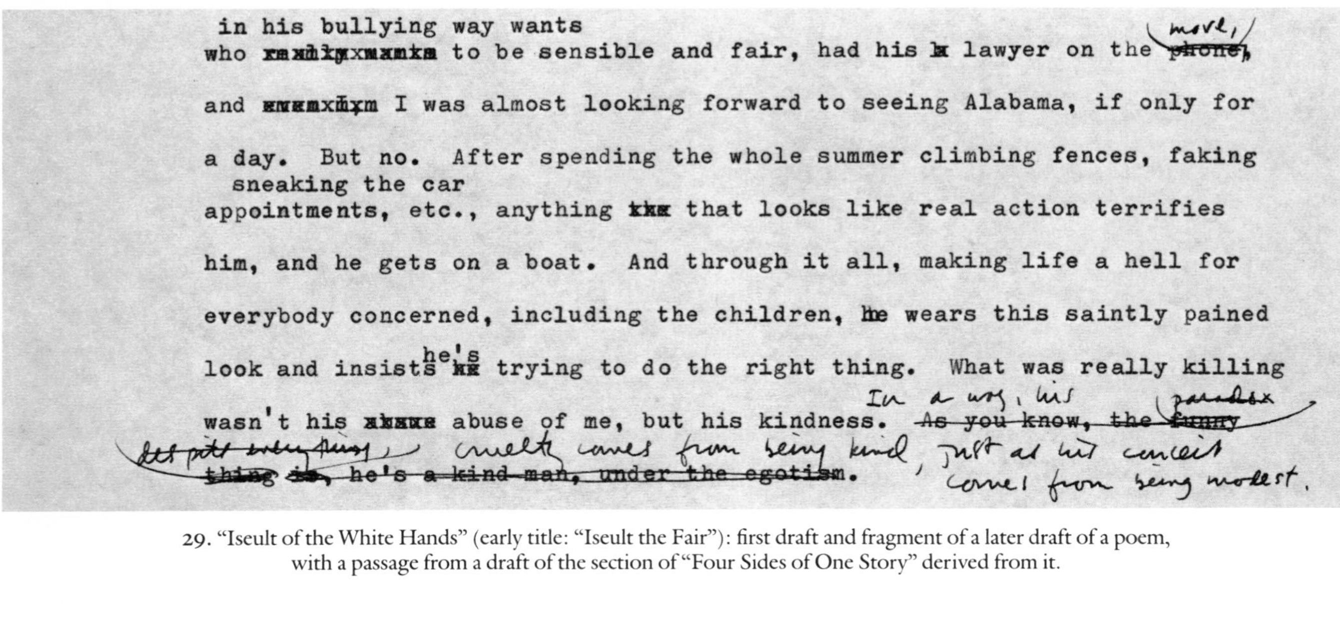
in his bullying way wants
who ~~xxxxxxxxxx~~ to be sensible and fair, had his ~~x~~ lawyer on the ~~phone,~~ move,

and ~~xxxxxx~~ I was almost looking forward to seeing Alabama, if only for

a day. But no. After spending the whole summer climbing fences, faking
sneaking the car
appointments, etc., anything ~~xxx~~ that looks like real action terrifies

him, and he gets on a boat. And through it all, making life a hell for

everybody concerned, including the children, ~~he~~ wears this saintly pained

look and insists he's ~~xx~~ trying to do the right thing. What was really killing

wasn't his ~~xxxxx~~ abuse of me, but his kindness. In a way, his ~~As you know, the~~ ~~funny~~ paradox
~~thing is, he's a kind man, under the egotism.~~ ~~despite everything,~~ cruelty comes from being kind, just as his conceit comes from being modest.

29. "Iseult of the White Hands" (early title: "Iseult the Fair"): first draft and fragment of a later draft of a poem, with a passage from a draft of the section of "Four Sides of One Story" derived from it.

The & John Updike

John

all years

John Updike

~~all years~~

~~held in his arms, I wanted to grow fat,~~

~~and sleep; He ravished me~~

I yearned to grow fat in his arms, and sleep,

But buy my ~~truth of gallantry~~, ~~all these~~

gallant fortune, enlarge

Our love at our expense, - He ravished me

to meet ~~wide~~ ~~toyed~~ emaciation not my stare

Because my face my heart my hands, my ~~eyes~~ pulse . . .

scattered wholly aching for his sword.

Iseult the Fair

My dearest Tristan--

Your letter confused and frightened me me -- I showed it to Mark --
he is thinking of suing you for alienation again -- pathetic --
his attempts to make himself matter. If he knew I was writing this he would kick me out of the house -- and he's right.

You say your body aches but you leave -- you enlarge our love at our expense -- I wanted to grow fat in your arms and sleep and you ravished me with doubts -- tore me apart with ~~absences.~~ withdrawals. (absences.) I have lost twelve pounds and never sleep -- my stare frightens people.

I must kill you in my heart -- I pray for your death and then for

12

I wanted to grow fat in your arms and sleep and you ravished me with absences -- tore me with doubts -- I have lost 12 pounds and live on pills -- I frighten myself.

Trist

Mr.

Mrs.

the flowers are gone and the books hidden and heavy winter here -- his knock on the door

29. "Iseult the Fair": first notes for a poem and passages from two drafts of the third section of "Four Sides of One Story."

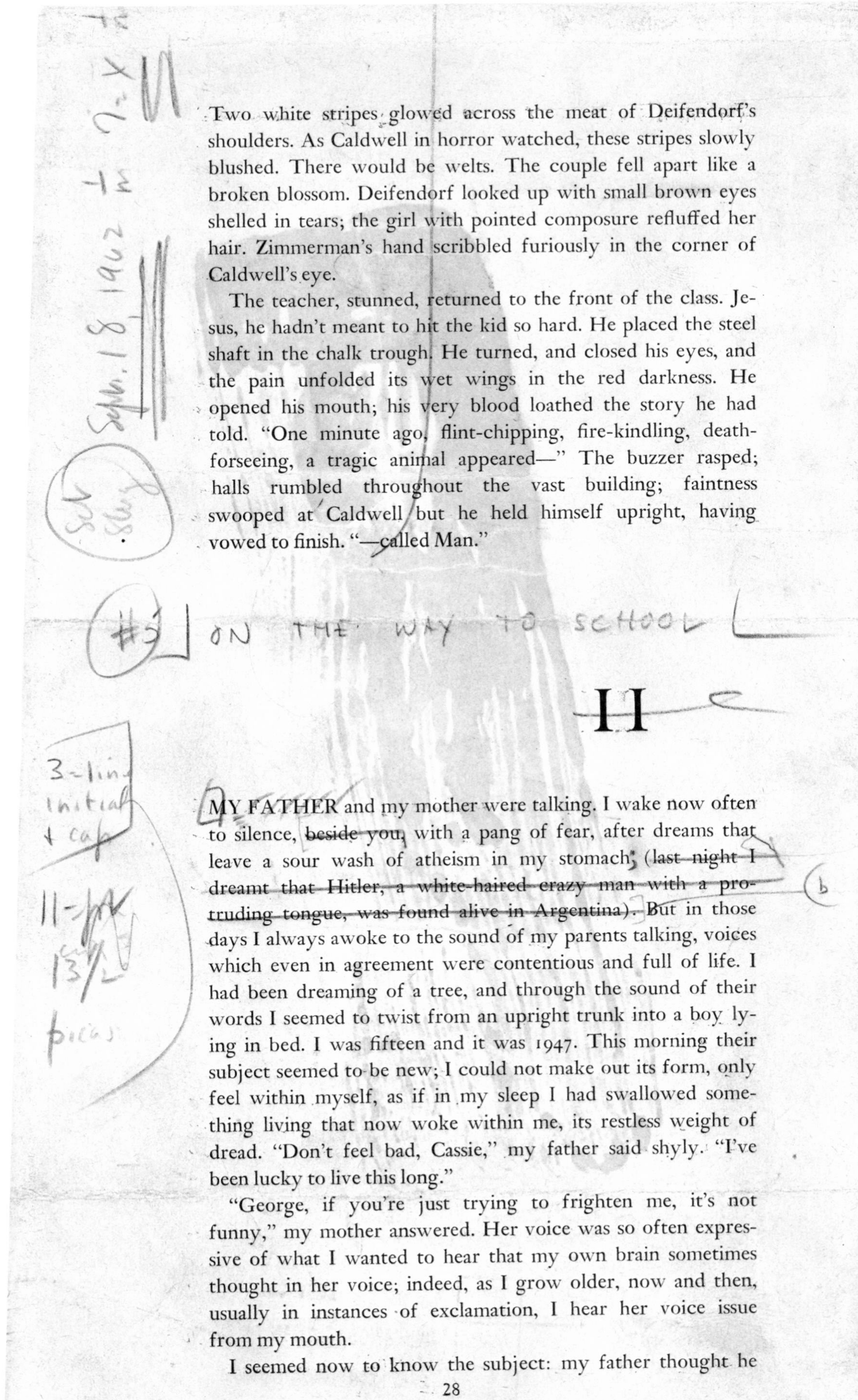

Two white stripes glowed across the meat of Deifendorf's shoulders. As Caldwell in horror watched, these stripes slowly blushed. There would be welts. The couple fell apart like a broken blossom. Deifendorf looked up with small brown eyes shelled in tears; the girl with pointed composure refluffed her hair. Zimmerman's hand scribbled furiously in the corner of Caldwell's eye.

The teacher, stunned, returned to the front of the class. Jesus, he hadn't meant to hit the kid so hard. He placed the steel shaft in the chalk trough. He turned, and closed his eyes, and the pain unfolded its wet wings in the red darkness. He opened his mouth; his very blood loathed the story he had told. "One minute ago, flint-chipping, fire-kindling, death-forseeing, a tragic animal appeared—" The buzzer rasped; halls rumbled throughout the vast building; faintness swooped at Caldwell but he held himself upright, having vowed to finish. "—called Man."

#5 ON THE WAY TO SCHOOL

II

MY FATHER and my mother were talking. I wake now often to silence, ~~beside you,~~ with a pang of fear, after dreams that leave a sour wash of atheism in my stomach; ~~(last night I dreamt that Hitler, a white-haired crazy man with a protruding tongue, was found alive in Argentina).~~ But in those days I always awoke to the sound of my parents talking, voices which even in agreement were contentious and full of life. I had been dreaming of a tree, and through the sound of their words I seemed to twist from an upright trunk into a boy lying in bed. I was fifteen and it was 1947. This morning their subject seemed to be new; I could not make out its form, only feel within myself, as if in my sleep I had swallowed something living that now woke within me, its restless weight of dread. "Don't feel bad, Cassie," my father said shyly. "I've been lucky to live this long."

"George, if you're just trying to frighten me, it's not funny," my mother answered. Her voice was so often expressive of what I wanted to hear that my own brain sometimes thought in her voice; indeed, as I grow older, now and then, usually in instances of exclamation, I hear her voice issue from my mouth.

I seemed now to know the subject: my father thought he

28

31. Part of Knopf galley of *The Centaur*, chapter II, revised as the working proof for the *New Yorker* short story "On the Way to School."

1/23/57

To: Mr. Updike

From: S

FOR USE ONLY WITH RUSH MESSAGES OR MATERIAL

Want to try it as an original?

T

oksk

Moon

Talk Fact

Although we did a Baedeker on the moon a number of years back (ten it turns out), we might try another. Both Russia and the United States are planning to lay claim to it. Russia feels it can do so by 1970 and the attached clip suggests a way that this country can beat that date. There are so many interesting facts about the moon that there would be no need for us to duplicate any that we used before, yet come up with quite a solid story.

Kinkead 1/21/57

REACHING FOR THE MOON: A proposal to claim the moon by planting an American flag by rocket has been made by a national science magazine. The suggested landing would be the first step in implementing President Eisenhower's idea for international control of interplanetary space and earth satellites. Russia has already announced plans to grab control of the moon by 1970 by use of radio-controlled rockets and "tank laboratories."

32. Cover memo from William Shawn suggesting a *New Yorker* "Talk of the Town" piece.

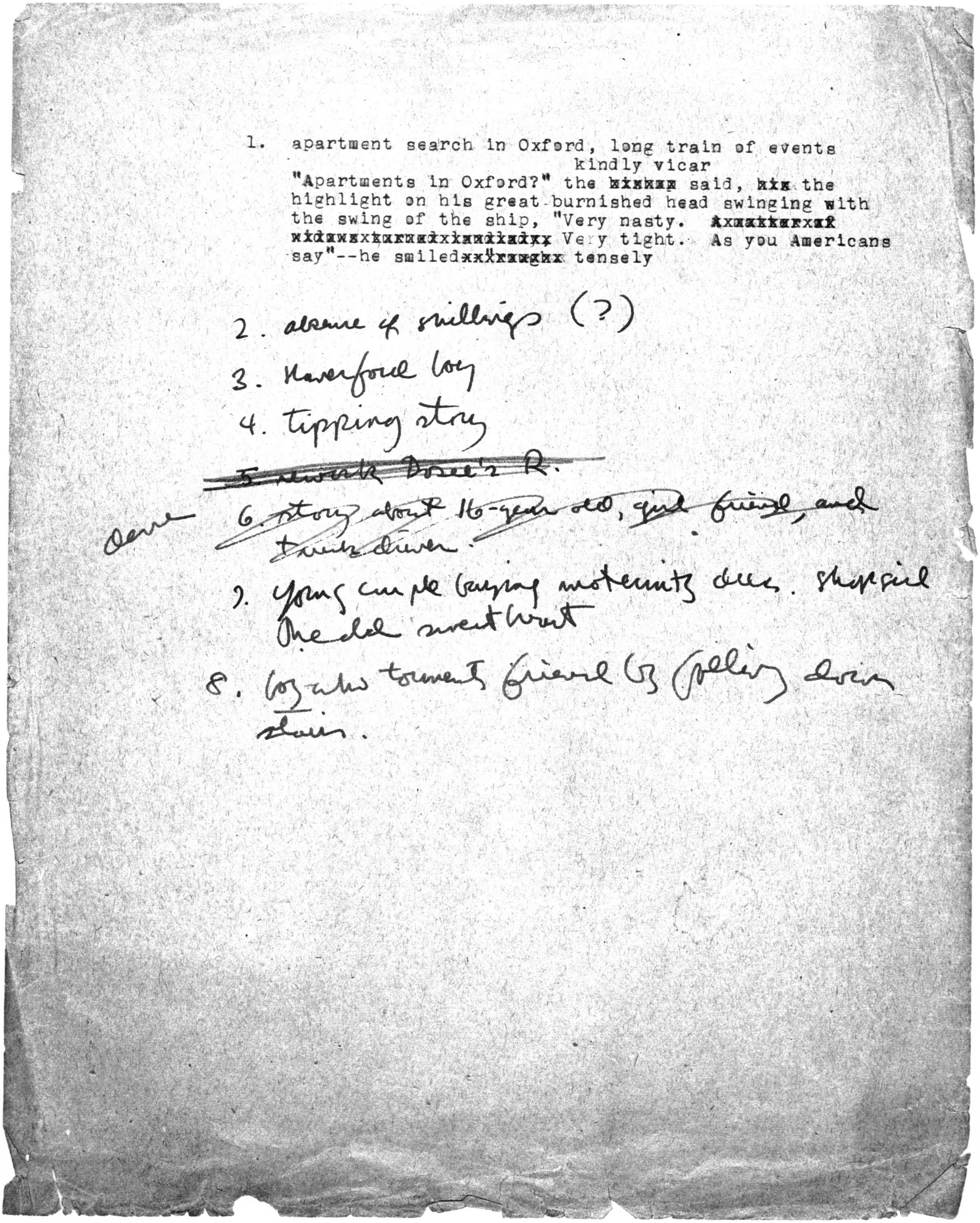

1. apartment search in Oxford, long train of events
kindly vicar
"Apartments in Oxford?" the ~~xxxxxx~~ said, ~~xxx~~ the highlight on his great burnished head swinging with the swing of the ship, "Very nasty. ~~xxxxxxxxxxxx xxxxxxxxxxxxxxxxxxxxxxxxxxx~~ Very tight. As you Americans say"--he smiled~~xxxxxxxxx~~ tensely

2. absence of shillings (?)

3. Haverford boy

4. tipping story

~~5. Newark Dosie's R.~~

done 6. ~~story about 16-year old, girl friend, and truck driver.~~

7. young couple buying maternity dress. shopgirl the old sweetheart

8. boy who torments friend by pulling down stairs.

34. List of story ideas, the first of which became "A Madman."

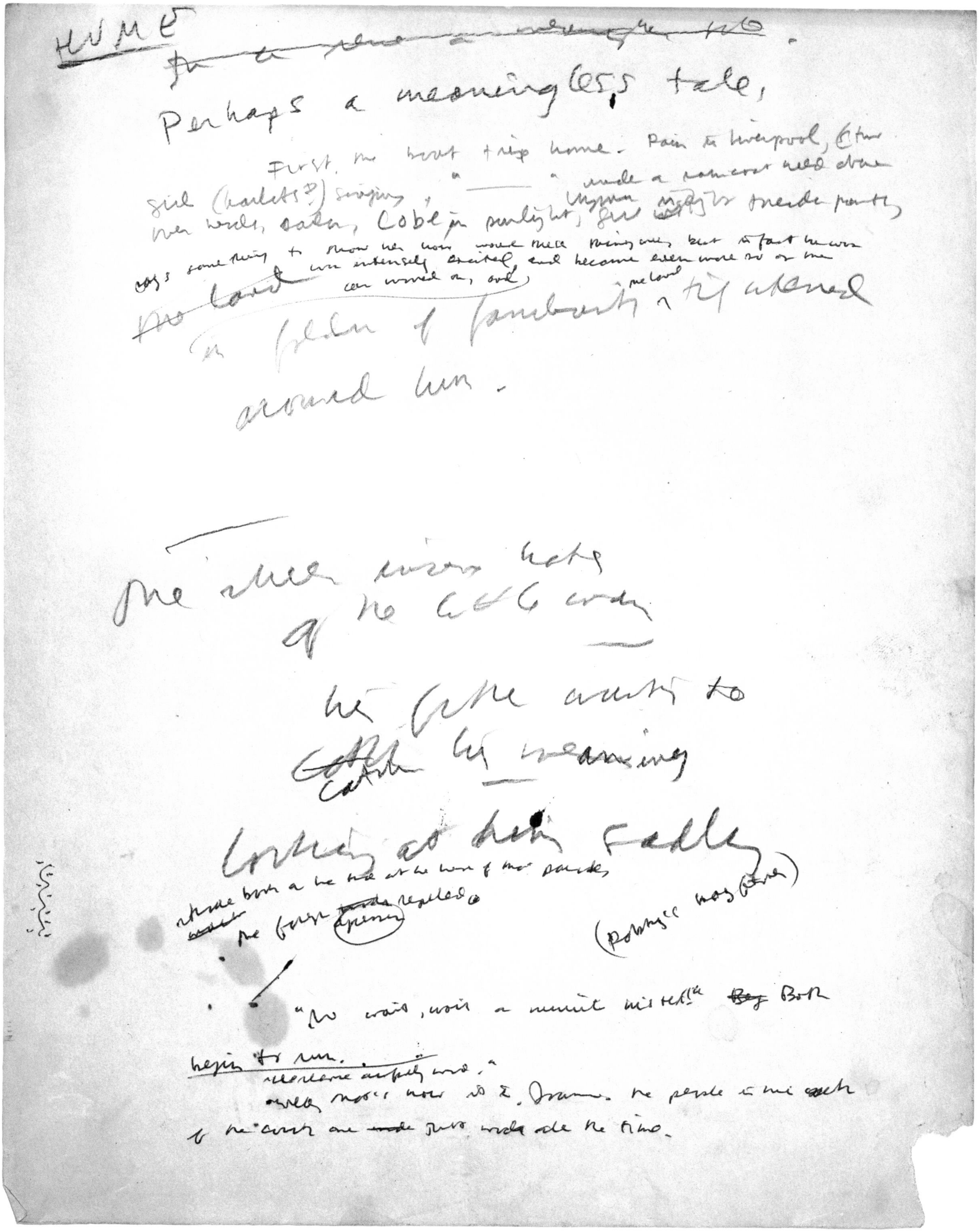

HOME

Perhaps a meaningless tale,

First, the boat trip home. Rain to Liverpool, [illegible]

[illegible]

around him.

[illegible]

"No wait, wait a minute mister!" Bob

[illegible]

36. Page of notes for the short story "Home," including the first and last words of the story.

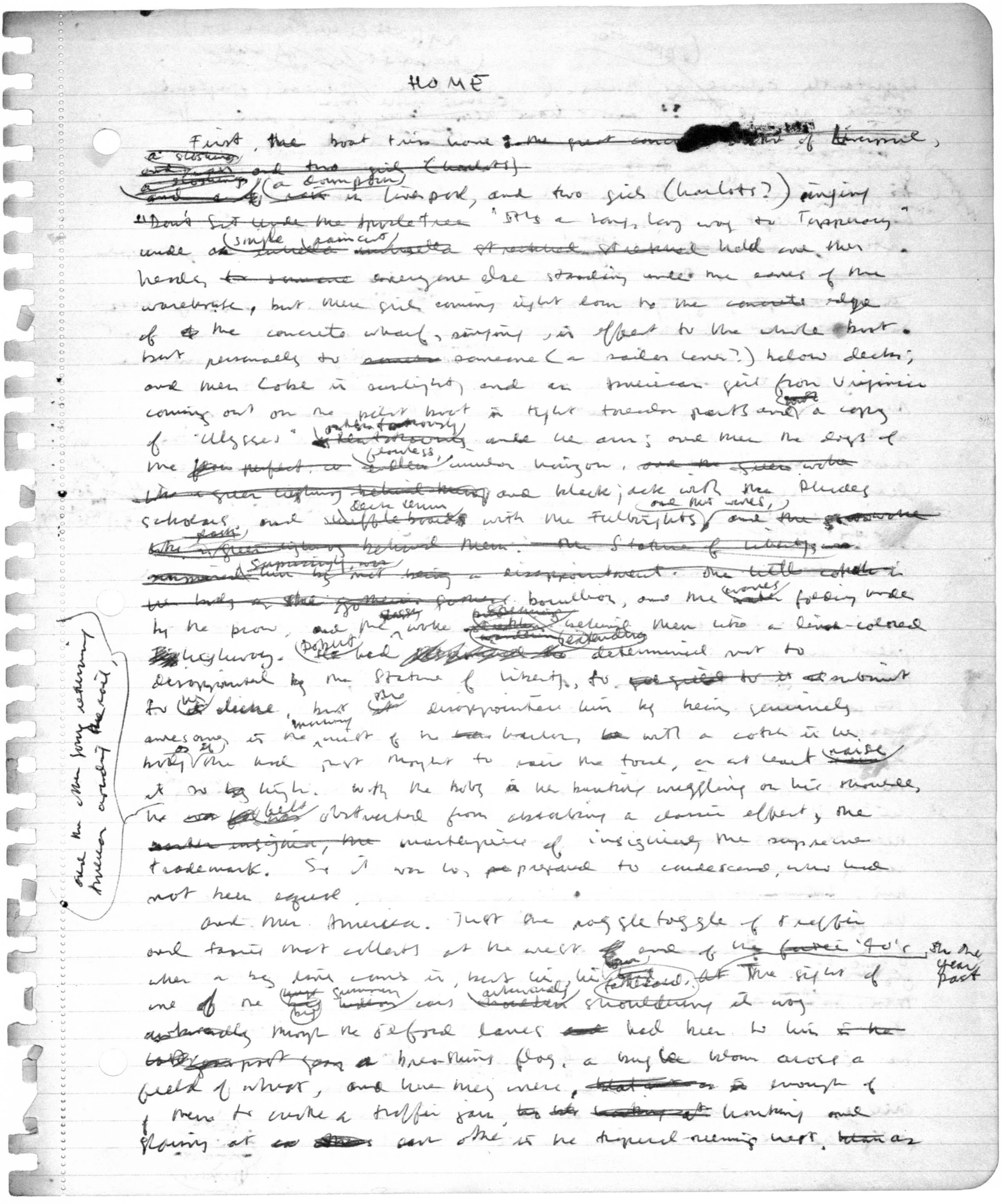

HOME

First, the boat tied home in Liverpool, and two girls (harlots?) singing "It's a long, long way to Tipperary" under a (simple raincoat) held over their heads, everyone else standing under the eaves of the warehouse, but these girls coming right down to the edge of the concrete wharf, singing in effect to the whole boat but personally to someone (a sailor lover?) below decks; and then Cobh in sunlight and an American girl from Virginia coming out on the pilot boat in tight toreador pants and a copy of "Ulysses" ostentatiously under her arm; and then the days of the flawless, [illegible] horizon, and blackjack with the Rhodes scholars and deck tennis with the Fulbrights (one not wives,) [illegible] bowsprit, and the waves folding under by the prow, and the glassy wake extending behind them into a lime-colored highway. Robert had determined not to be disappointed by the Statue of Liberty, to submit to its cliché, but she disappointed him by being genuinely awesome in the morning mist of the harbor, with a torch in her holy hand just bright enough to raise the tone, or at least raise it so high. With the baby in the bunting wriggling on his shoulder, he was obstructed from assaulting a [illegible] elbow, the masterpiece of insignia, the supreme trademark. So it was he, prepared to condescend, who had not been equal.

And then America. Just the raggle-taggle of traffic and faces that collects at the wharf [illegible] '40's when a big liner comes in, but [illegible]. The sight of one of the big summer cars awkwardly shouldering its way through the Oxford lanes had been to him a breathing flag, a bugle blown across a field of wheat, and here they were, enough of them to create a traffic jam, honking and glaring at each other in the tropical-seeming heat,

36. First page of first draft of "Home."

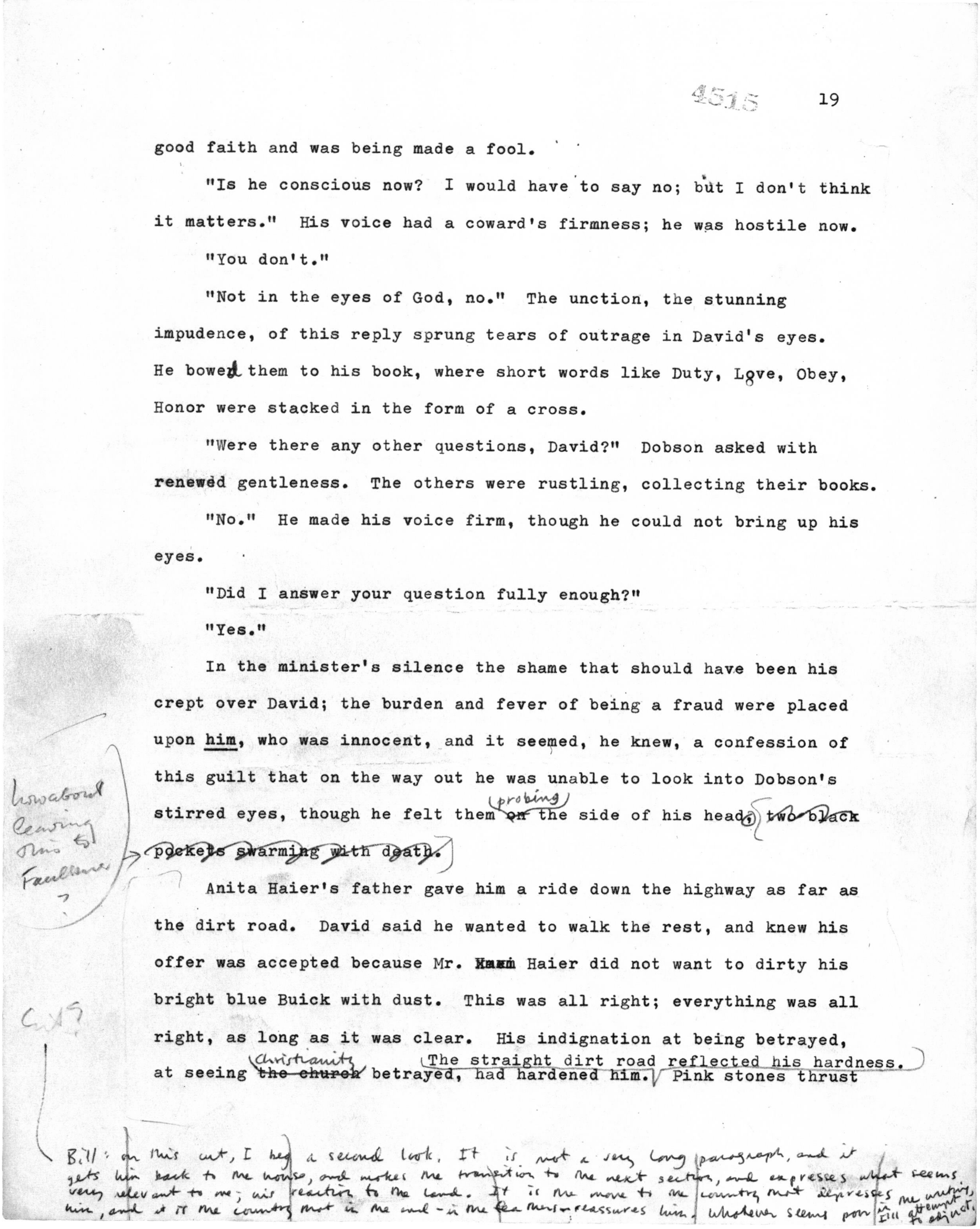
4515 19

good faith and was being made a fool.

"Is he conscious now? I would have to say no; but I don't think it matters." His voice had a coward's firmness; he was hostile now.

"You don't."

"Not in the eyes of God, no." The unction, the stunning impudence, of this reply sprung tears of outrage in David's eyes. He bowed them to his book, where short words like Duty, Love, Obey, Honor were stacked in the form of a cross.

"Were there any other questions, David?" Dobson asked with renewed gentleness. The others were rustling, collecting their books.

"No." He made his voice firm, though he could not bring up his eyes.

"Did I answer your question fully enough?"

"Yes."

In the minister's silence the shame that should have been his crept over David; the burden and fever of being a fraud were placed upon <u>him</u>, who was innocent, and it seemed, he knew, a confession of this guilt that on the way out he was unable to look into Dobson's stirred eyes, though he felt them ~~on~~ probing the side of his head. ~~two black pockets swarming with death.~~

how about leaving this to Faulkner?

Anita Haier's father gave him a ride down the highway as far as the dirt road. David said he wanted to walk the rest, and knew his offer was accepted because Mr. ~~Haxm~~ Haier did not want to dirty his bright blue Buick with dust. This was all right; everything was all right, as long as it was clear. His indignation at being betrayed, at seeing ~~the church~~ Christianity betrayed, had hardened him. The straight dirt road reflected his hardness. Pink stones thrust

Cut?

Bill: on this cut, I beg a second look. It is not a very long paragraph, and it gets him back to the house, and makes the transition to the next section, and expresses what seems very relevant to me; his reaction to the land. It is the move to the country that depresses him, and it is the country that in the end – in the feathers – reassures him. Whatever seems poor in the writing, I'll attempt to adjust.

37. Page of *New Yorker* printer's copy of "Pigeon Feathers" including annotations by William Maxwell and the author concerning a suggested cut.

G NYr A—239

5556—ELEVEN

luck must ride with the ball. Three innings before, we had seen a brave effort fail. Nevertheless, there always will lurk, around a corner in a pocket of our knowledge of the odds, an indefensible hope, and this was one of the times, which you now and then find in sports, when a density of expectation hangs in the air and plucks an event out of the future.

Fisher, after his unsettling wait, was wide with the first pitch. He put the second one over, and Wiliams swung mightily, and th crowd grunted, seeing that classic swing, so long and smooth and quick, exposed, naked and graceful in its failure. Fisher threw the third time, Williams swung again, and there it was.

It was in the books while it was still in the sky. The ball climbed on a diagonal line into the vast volume of air over center field. From my angle, behind third base, the ball seemed less an object in flight than the tip of a towering, motionless construct, like the Eiffel Tower or the Tappan Zee Bridge. Brandt ran back to the deepest corner of outfield grass; the ball ~~descended~~ and struck in the crotch where the ~~visitors'~~ bullpen met the wall, ~~bounced chunkily, and vanished. It was~~ a few yards to the right of the 420-foot sign. It was quite near to where he hit his first home run in 1939.

Like a feather caught in a vortex, Williams ran around the square of bases at the center of our beseeching screaming. He ran as he always ran out home runs—hurriedly, unsmiling, head down, as if our praise was a storm of rain to get out of. He didn't tip his hat. Though we thumped, wept, and chanted "We Want Ted" for minutes after he hid in the dugout, he did not come back. Our noise for some seconds passed beyond excitement into a kind of immense open anguish, a wailing, a cry to be saved. But immortality is nontransferable. The papers said that the other players and even the umpires on the field begged him to come out and acknowledge us in some way, but he never had and did not now. Gods do not answer letters.

EVERY true story has an anticlimax; the players on the field refused to vanish, as would have seemed decent, in the smoke of Williams' miracle. Fisher continued to pitch, and escaped further harm. At the end of the inning, Higgins sent Williams out to his left-field position, then instantly replaced him with Carol Hardy, so we had a long last look at Williams as he jogged out there and then back, all the while staring at the ground. It was nice, and we were grateful, but it left a funny taste.

One of the scholiasts behind me said, "Let's go. We've seen everything. I don't want to spoil it." This seemed sound aesthetic decision. Williams' last word had been so exquisitely chosen, such a perfect fusing of expectation, intention, and execution, that already it felt a little unreal in my head, and I

This ball did hit over the roof of the bullpen shelter and did count as a home run. However: it didn't vanish. Red Sox info. says that it fell back into the field and was thrown in by Oriole outfielder Pilarcik.

rr]

[illegible]

[home/club

sailed over his head, ~~too~~ struck.

dribbled back onto the field, offering itself to the Hall of Fame as a souvenir.

39. *New Yorker* galley of "Hub Fans Bid Kid Adieu," including (left) annotation by a "checker" and (right) the author's subsequent revision.

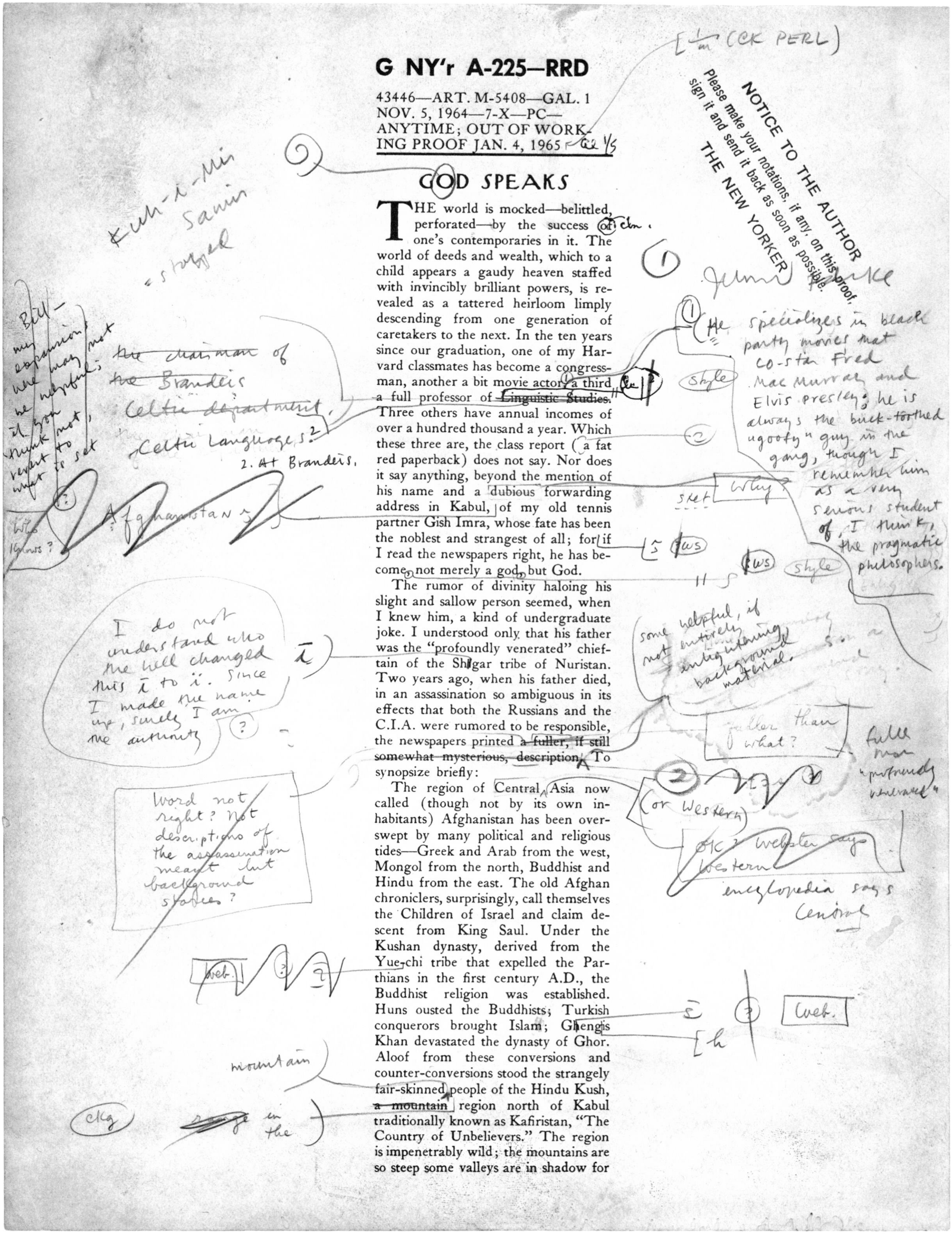

G NY'r A-225—RRD

43446—ART. M-5408—GAL. 1
NOV. 5, 1964—7-X—PC—
ANYTIME; OUT OF WORKING PROOF JAN. 4, 1965

NOTICE TO THE AUTHOR
Please make your notations, if any, on this proof, sign it and send it back as soon as possible.
THE NEW YORKER

GOD SPEAKS

THE world is mocked—belittled, perforated—by the success of one's contemporaries in it. The world of deeds and wealth, which to a child appears a gaudy heaven staffed with invincibly brilliant powers, is revealed as a tattered heirloom limply descending from one generation of caretakers to the next. In the ten years since our graduation, one of my Harvard classmates has become a congressman, another a bit movie actor, a third a full professor of ~~Linguistic Studies~~. Three others have annual incomes of over a hundred thousand a year. Which these three are, the class report (a fat red paperback) does not say. Nor does it say anything, beyond the mention of his name and a dubious forwarding address in Kabul, of my old tennis partner Gish Imra, whose fate has been the noblest and strangest of all; for if I read the newspapers right, he has become, not merely a god, but God.

The rumor of divinity haloing his slight and sallow person seemed, when I knew him, a kind of undergraduate joke. I understood only that his father was the "profoundly venerated" chieftain of the Shigar tribe of Nuristan. Two years ago, when his father died, in an assassination so ambiguous in its effects that both the Russians and the C.I.A. were rumored to be responsible, the newspapers printed ~~a fuller, if still somewhat mysterious, description~~. To synopsize briefly:

The region of Central Asia now called (though not by its own inhabitants) Afghanistan has been overswept by many political and religious tides—Greek and Arab from the west, Mongol from the north, Buddhist and Hindu from the east. The old Afghan chroniclers, surprisingly, call themselves the Children of Israel and claim descent from King Saul. Under the Kushan dynasty, derived from the Yue-chi tribe that expelled the Parthians in the first century A.D., the Buddhist religion was established. Huns ousted the Buddhists; Turkish conquerors brought Islam; Ghengis Khan devastated the dynasty of Ghor. Aloof from these conversions and counter-conversions stood the strangely fair-skinned people of the Hindu Kush, ~~a mountain~~ region north of Kabul traditionally known as Kafiristan, "The Country of Unbelievers." The region is impenetrably wild; the mountains are so steep some valleys are in shadow for

41. *New Yorker* galley of "God Speaks," which a "checker," William Maxwell, and the author have annotated on questions of style, spelling, and geography.

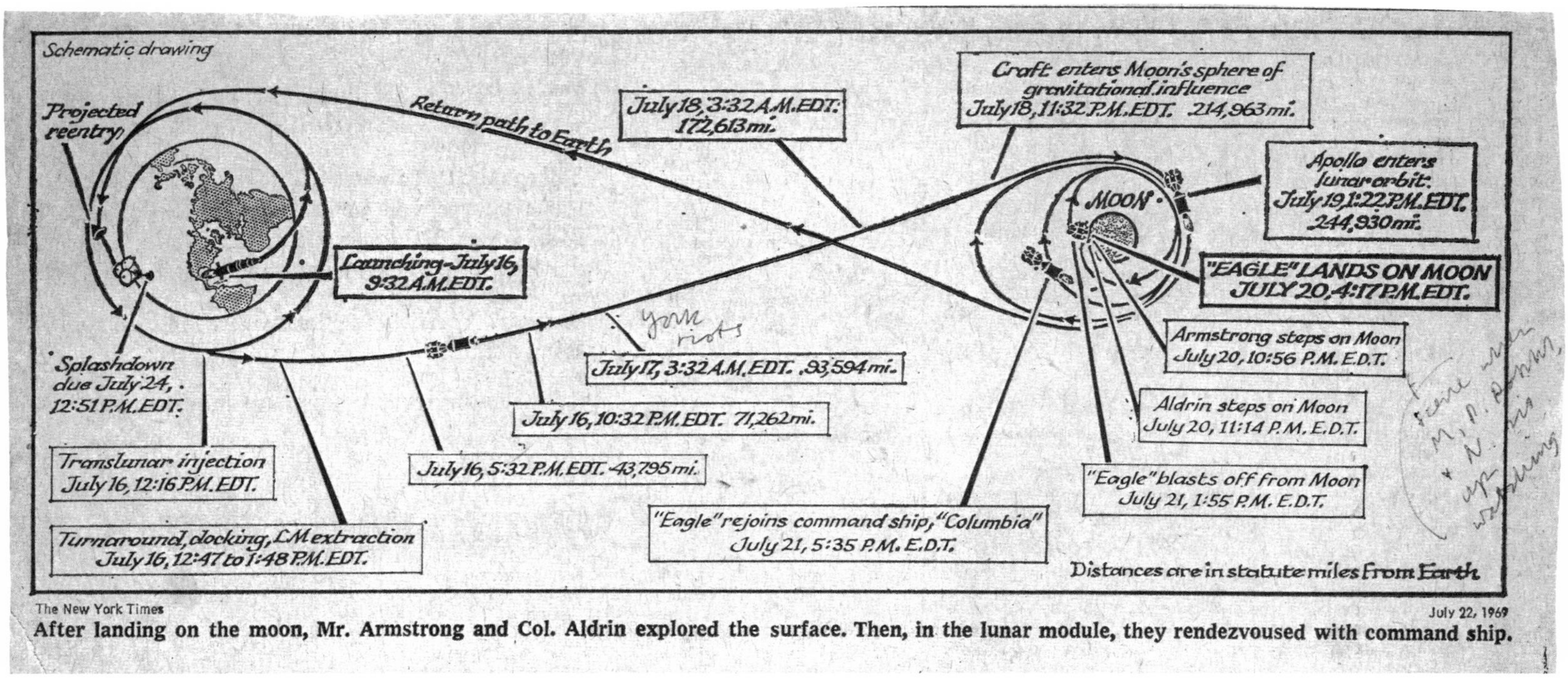

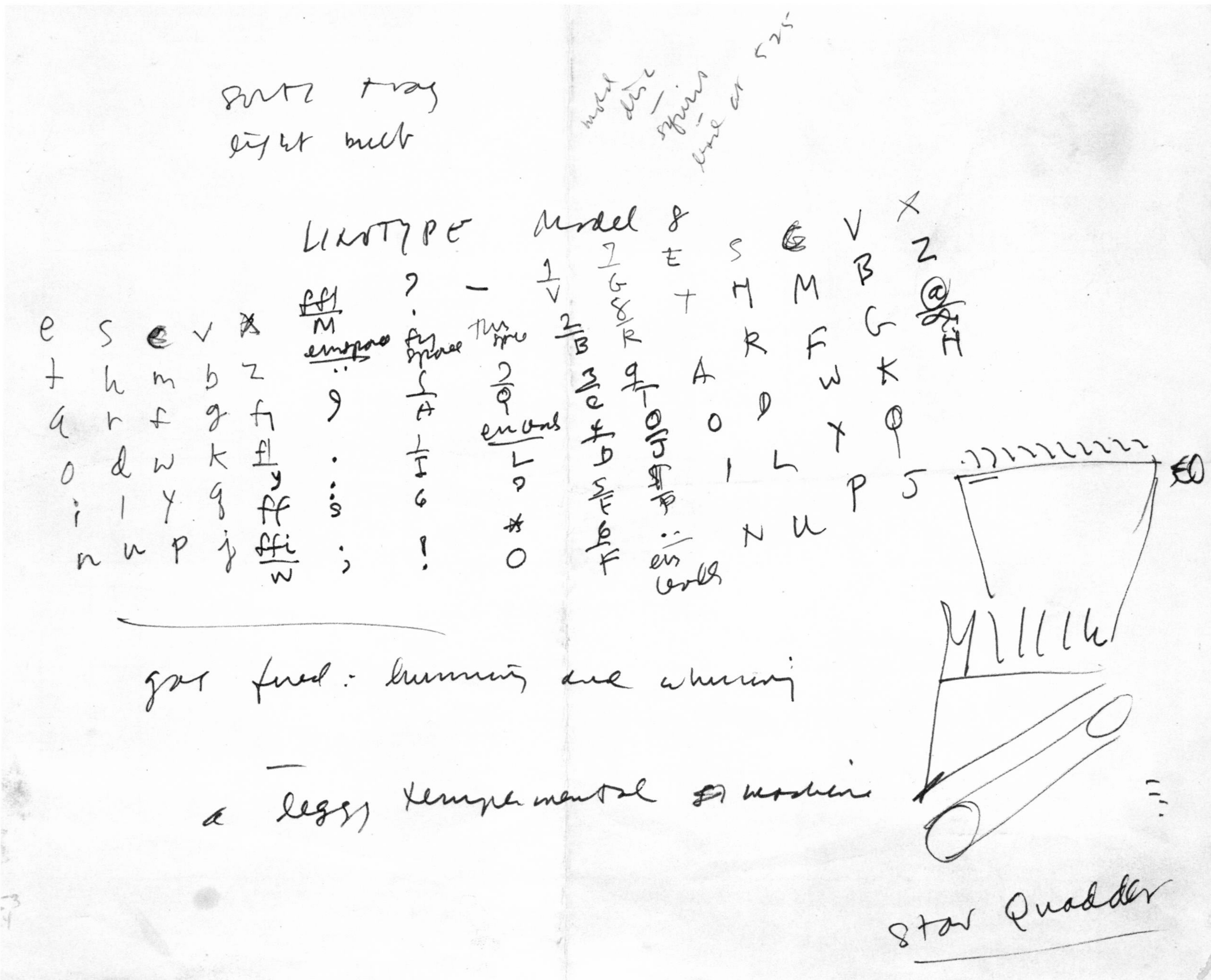

44. Clipping of *New York Times* diagram of the 1969 Apollo space flight, annotated with chronology of some events in *Rabbit Redux*, and diagram of linotype sorts tray.

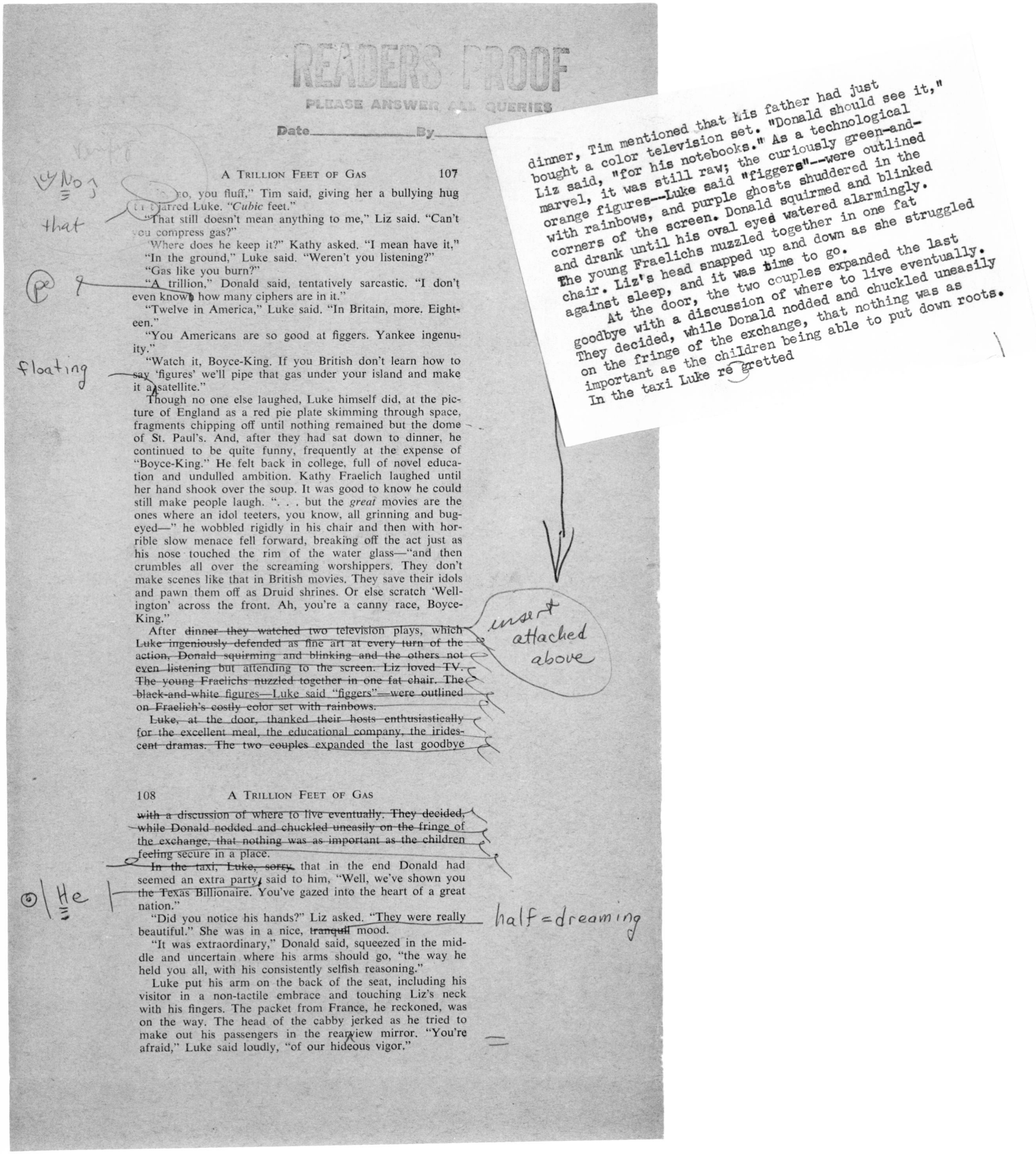
READERS PROOF
PLEASE ANSWER ALL QUERIES
Date ______ By ______

A Trillion Feet of Gas 107

"[No,] no, you fluff," Tim said, giving her a bullying hug [that] jarred Luke. "*Cubic* feet."

"That still doesn't mean anything to me," Liz said. "Can't you compress gas?"

"Where does he keep it?" Kathy asked. "I mean have it,"

"In the ground," Luke said. "Weren't you listening?"

"Gas like you burn?"

"A trillion," Donald said, tentatively sarcastic. "I don't even know how many ciphers are in it."

"Twelve in America," Luke said. "In Britain, more. Eighteen."

"You Americans are so good at figgers. Yankee ingenuity."

"Watch it, Boyce-King. If you British don't learn how to say 'figures' we'll pipe that gas under your island and make it a satellite."

Though no one else laughed, Luke himself did, at the picture of England as a red pie plate skimming through space, fragments chipping off until nothing remained but the dome of St. Paul's. And, after they had sat down to dinner, he continued to be quite funny, frequently at the expense of "Boyce-King." He felt back in college, full of novel education and undulled ambition. Kathy Fraelich laughed until her hand shook over the soup. It was good to know he could still make people laugh. ". . . but the *great* movies are the ones where an idol teeters, you know, all grinning and bug-eyed—" he wobbled rigidly in his chair and then with horrible slow menace fell forward, breaking off the act just as his nose touched the rim of the water glass—"and then crumbles all over the screaming worshippers. They don't make scenes like that in British movies. They save their idols and pawn them off as Druid shrines. Or else scratch 'Wellington' across the front. Ah, you're a canny race, Boyce-King."

After ~~dinner they watched two television plays, which Luke ingeniously defended as fine art at every turn of the action, Donald squirming and blinking and the others not even listening but attending to the screen. Liz loved TV. The young Fraelichs nuzzled together in one fat chair. The black-and-white figures—Luke said "figgers"—were outlined on Fraelich's costly color set with rainbows.~~

~~Luke, at the door, thanked their hosts enthusiastically for the excellent meal, the educational company, the iridescent dramas. The two couples expanded the last goodbye~~

108 A Trillion Feet of Gas

~~with a discussion of where to live eventually. They decided, while Donald nodded and chuckled uneasily on the fringe of the exchange, that nothing was as important as the children feeling secure in a place.~~

~~In the taxi, Luke, sorry~~ that in the end Donald had seemed an extra party, said to him, "Well, we've shown you the Texas Billionaire. You've gazed into the heart of a great nation."

"Did you notice his hands?" Liz asked. "They were really beautiful." She was in a nice, ~~tranquil~~ mood.

"It was extraordinary," Donald said, squeezed in the middle and uncertain where his arms should go, "the way he held you all, with his consistently selfish reasoning."

Luke put his arm on the back of the seat, including his visitor in a non-tactile embrace and touching Liz's neck with his fingers. The packet from France, he reckoned, was on the way. The head of the cabby jerked as he tried to make out his passengers in the rearview mirror. "You're afraid," Luke said loudly, "of our hideous vigor."

that
floating
He
half=dreaming
insert attached above
dinner, Tim mentioned that his father had just bought a color television set. "Donald should see it," Liz said, "for his notebooks." As a technological marvel, it was still raw; the curiously green-and-orange figures--Luke said "figgers"--were outlined with rainbows, and purple ghosts shuddered in the corners of the screen. Donald squirmed and blinked and drank until his oval eyes watered alarmingly. The young Fraelichs nuzzled together in one fat chair. Liz's head snapped up and down as she struggled against sleep, and it was time to go.
At the door, the two couples expanded the last goodbye with a discussion of where to live eventually. They decided, while Donald nodded and chuckled uneasily on the fringe of the exchange, that nothing was as important as the children being able to put down roots. In the taxi Luke regretted

49. Uncut page proof of *The Same Door*, including revisions for Fawcett-Crest edition.

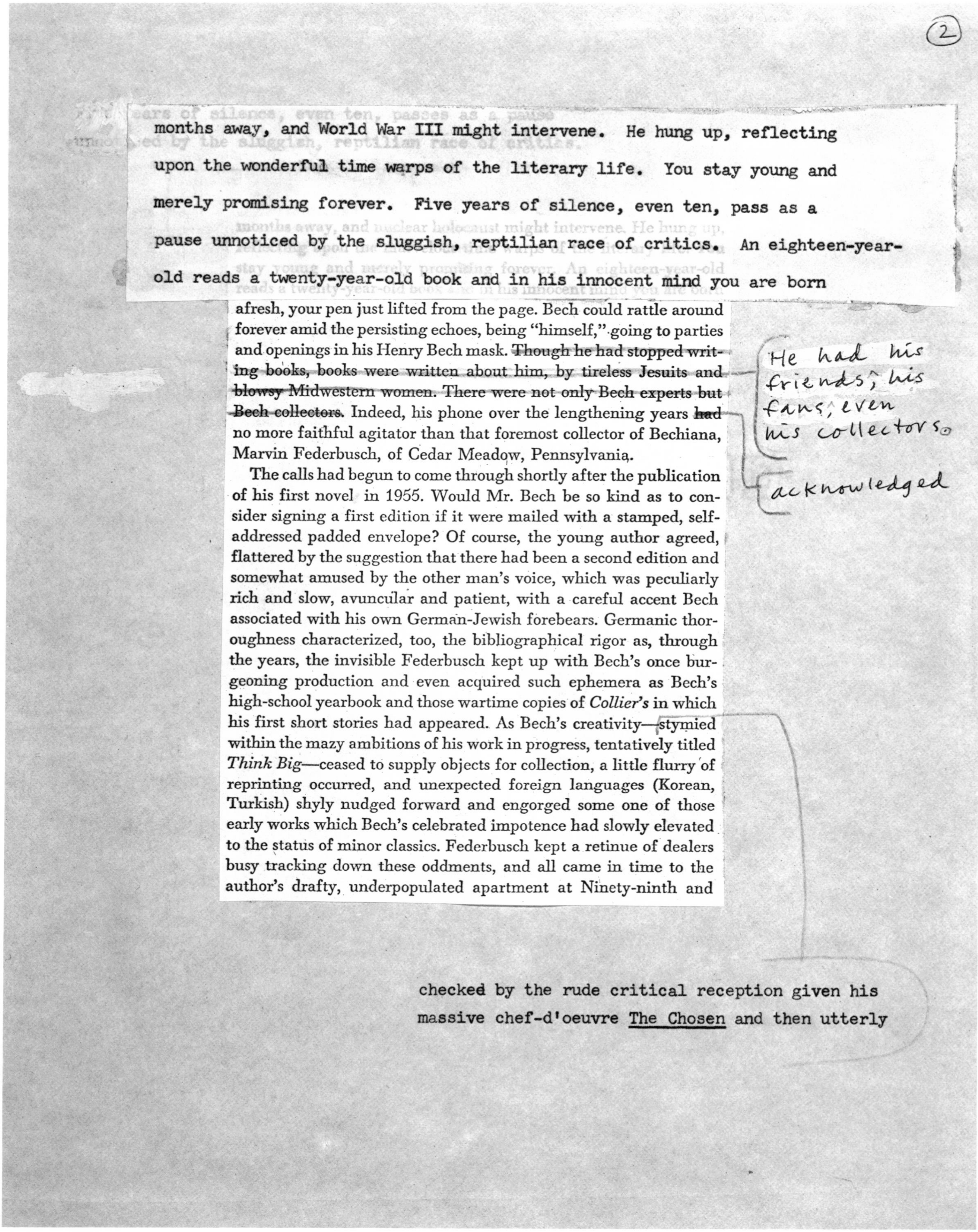

2

months away, and World War III might intervene. He hung up, reflecting upon the wonderful time warps of the literary life. You stay young and merely promising forever. Five years of silence, even ten, pass as a pause unnoticed by the sluggish, reptilian race of critics. An eighteen-year-old reads a twenty-year-old book and in his innocent mind you are born afresh, your pen just lifted from the page. Bech could rattle around forever amid the persisting echoes, being "himself," going to parties and openings in his Henry Bech mask. ~~Though he had stopped writing books, books were written about him, by tireless Jesuits and blowsy Midwestern women. There were not only Bech experts but Bech collectors.~~ Indeed, his phone over the lengthening years ~~had~~ no more faithful agitator than that foremost collector of Bechiana, Marvin Federbusch, of Cedar Meadow, Pennsylvania.

He had his friends; his fans; even his collectors.

acknowledged

The calls had begun to come through shortly after the publication of his first novel in 1955. Would Mr. Bech be so kind as to consider signing a first edition if it were mailed with a stamped, self-addressed padded envelope? Of course, the young author agreed, flattered by the suggestion that there had been a second edition and somewhat amused by the other man's voice, which was peculiarly rich and slow, avuncular and patient, with a careful accent Bech associated with his own German-Jewish forebears. Germanic thoroughness characterized, too, the bibliographical rigor as, through the years, the invisible Federbusch kept up with Bech's once burgeoning production and even acquired such ephemera as Bech's high-school yearbook and those wartime copies of *Collier's* in which his first short stories had appeared. As Bech's creativity—stymied within the mazy ambitions of his work in progress, tentatively titled *Think Big*—ceased to supply objects for collection, a little flurry of reprinting occurred, and unexpected foreign languages (Korean, Turkish) shyly nudged forward and engorged some one of those early works which Bech's celebrated impotence had slowly elevated to the status of minor classics. Federbusch kept a retinue of dealers busy tracking down these oddments, and all came in time to the author's drafty, underpopulated apartment at Ninety-ninth and

checked by the rude critical reception given his massive chef-d'oeuvre The Chosen and then utterly

51. Printer's copy of a page for the collection *Bech is Back:* a page of the previously printed *Three Illuminations in the Life of an American Author* pasted up and annotated with revisions.

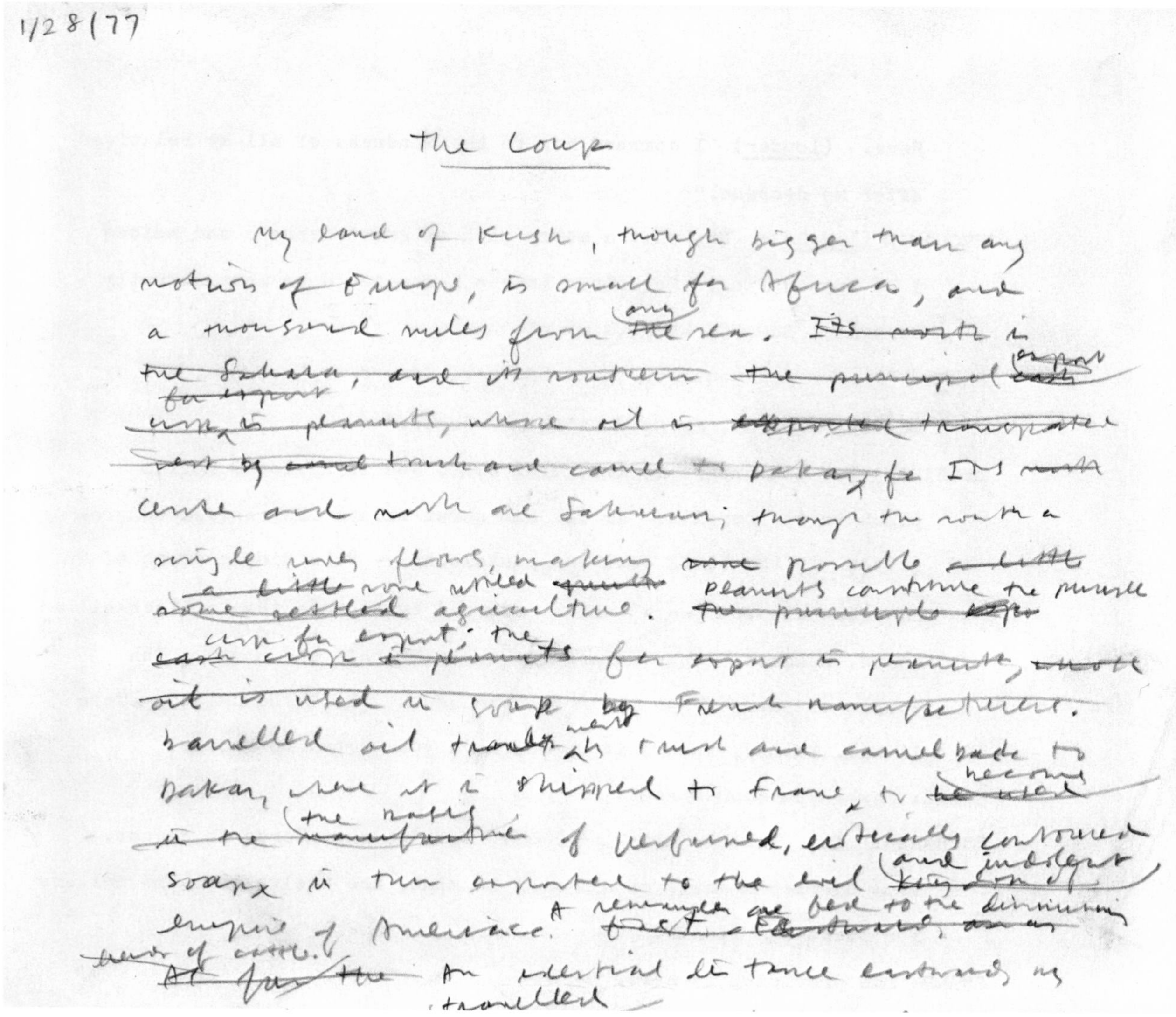

1/28/77

The Coup

My land of Kush, though bigger than any nation of Europe, is small for Africa, and a thousand miles from any sea. Its centre and north are Saharan; though the south a single river flows, making possible some settled agriculture. Peanuts constitute the principal crop for export; the barrelled oil travels west by truck and camelback to Dakar, where it is shipped to France, to become the basis of perfumed, erotically contoured soaps in turn exported to the evil and indulgent empire of America. A remainder are fed to the diminishing herds of cattle. An identical distance eastwards, my travelled

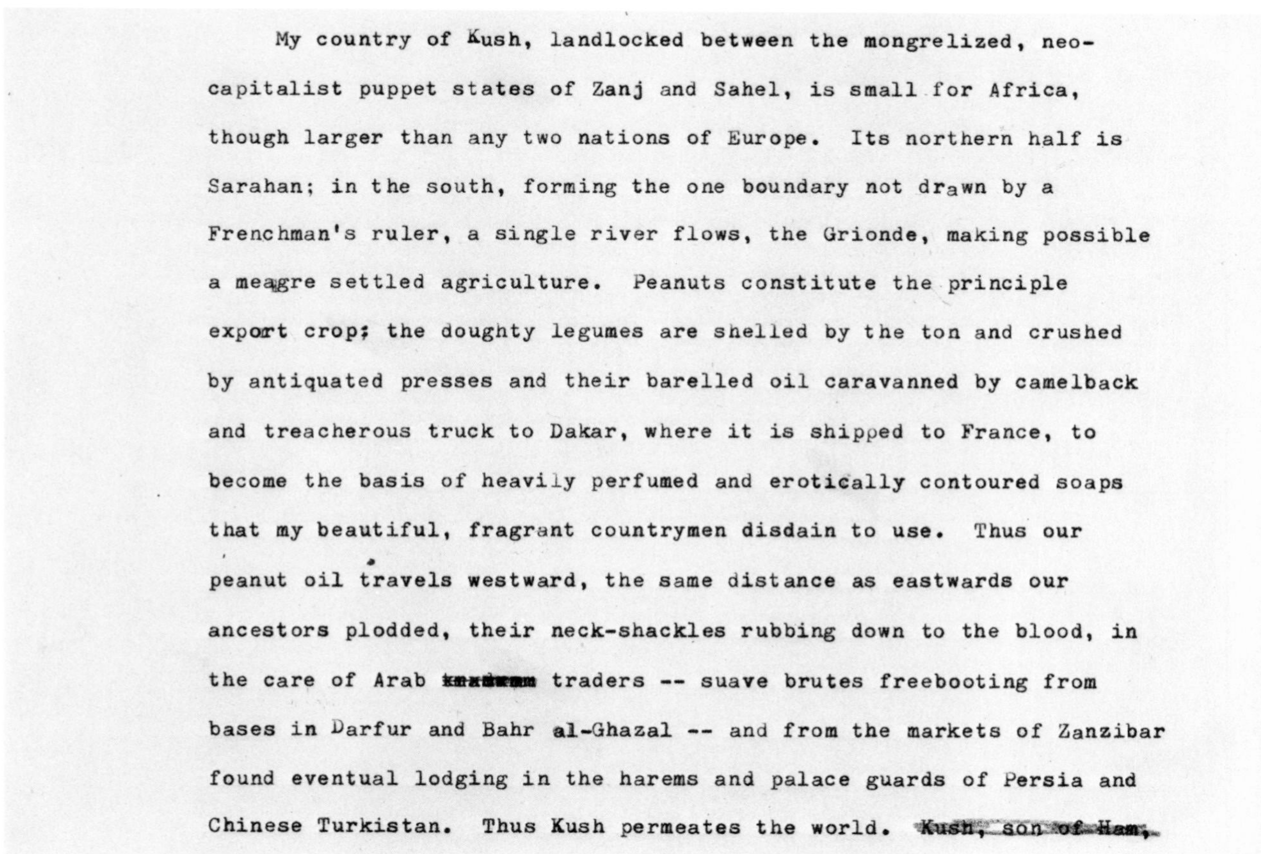

My country of Kush, landlocked between the mongrelized, neo-capitalist puppet states of Zanj and Sahel, is small for Africa, though larger than any two nations of Europe. Its northern half is Sarahan; in the south, forming the one boundary not drawn by a Frenchman's ruler, a single river flows, the Grionde, making possible a meagre settled agriculture. Peanuts constitute the principle export crop; the doughty legumes are shelled by the ton and crushed by antiquated presses and their barelled oil caravanned by camelback and treacherous truck to Dakar, where it is shipped to France, to become the basis of heavily perfumed and erotically contoured soaps that my beautiful, fragrant countrymen disdain to use. Thus our peanut oil travels westward, the same distance as eastwards our ancestors plodded, their neck-shackles rubbing down to the blood, in the care of Arab [redacted] traders -- suave brutes freebooting from bases in Darfur and Bahr al-Ghazal -- and from the markets of Zanzibar found eventual lodging in the harems and palace guards of Persia and Chinese Turkistan. Thus Kush permeates the world. ~~Kush, son of Ham,~~

55. Sections of first pages from an early and a later draft of *The Coup*.

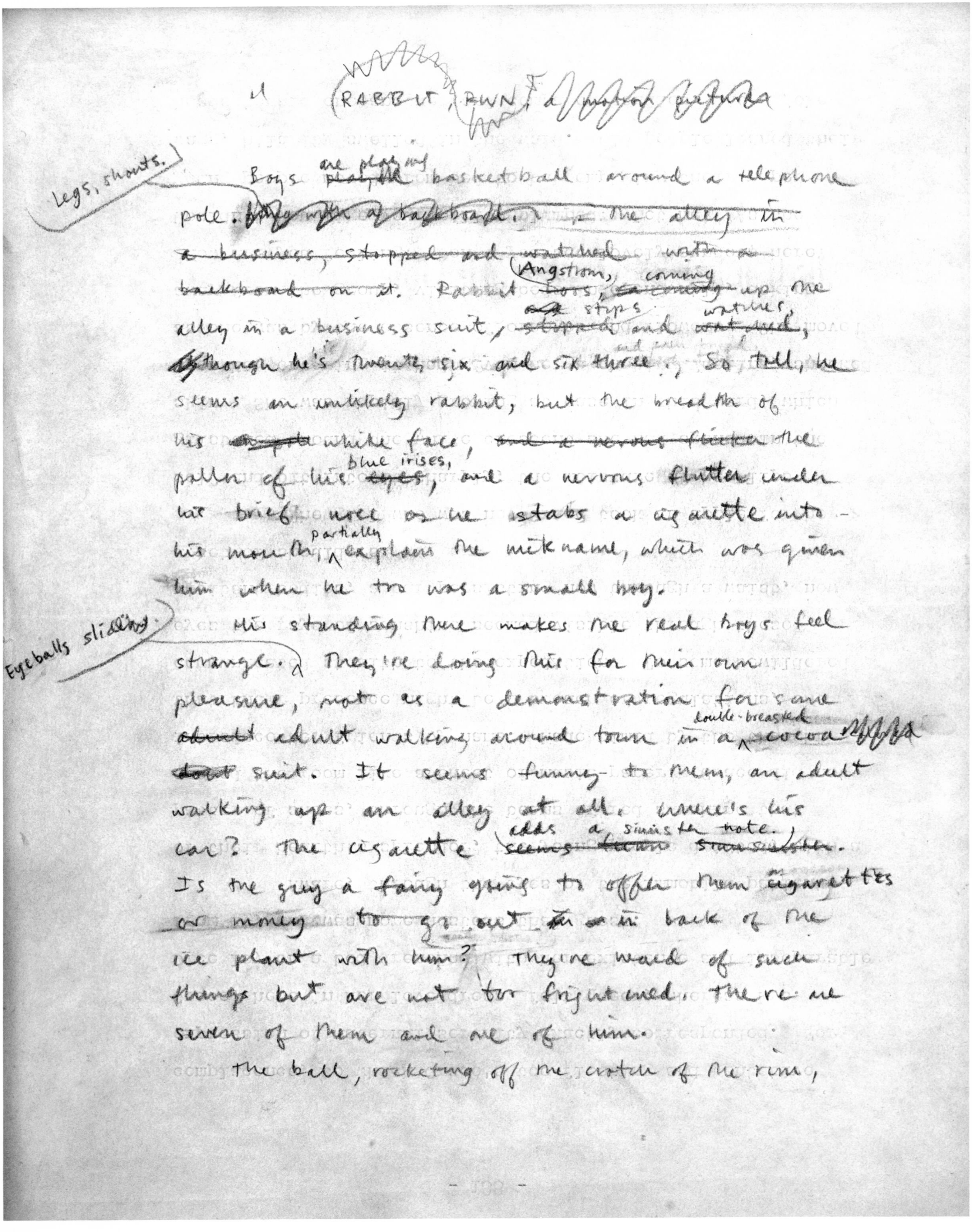

RABBIT, RUN, a movie in prose

Legs, shouts.

Boys are playing basketball around a telephone pole. ~~with a backboard.~~ ~~The alley in a business, stopped and watched with a backboard on it.~~ Rabbit Angstrom, ~~boss,~~ coming up the alley in a business suit, stops and watches, though he's twenty-six and six three. So tall, he seems an unlikely rabbit, but the breadth of his white face, the pallor of his blue irises, and a nervous flutter under his brief nose as he stabs a cigarette into his mouth, partially explain the nickname, which was given him when he too was a small boy.

Eyeballs sliding

His standing there makes the real boys feel strange. They're doing this for their own pleasure, not as a demonstration for some ~~adult~~ adult walking around town in a double-breasted cocoa suit. It seems funny to them, an adult walking up an alley at all. Where's his car? The cigarette adds a sinister note. Is the guy a fairy going to offer them cigarettes or money to go out in back of the ice plant with him? They've heard of such things but are not too frightened. There're seven of them and one of him.

The ball, rocketing off the crotch of the rim,

- 100 -

64. First page of an early draft of *Rabbit, Run*, indicating changes in title.

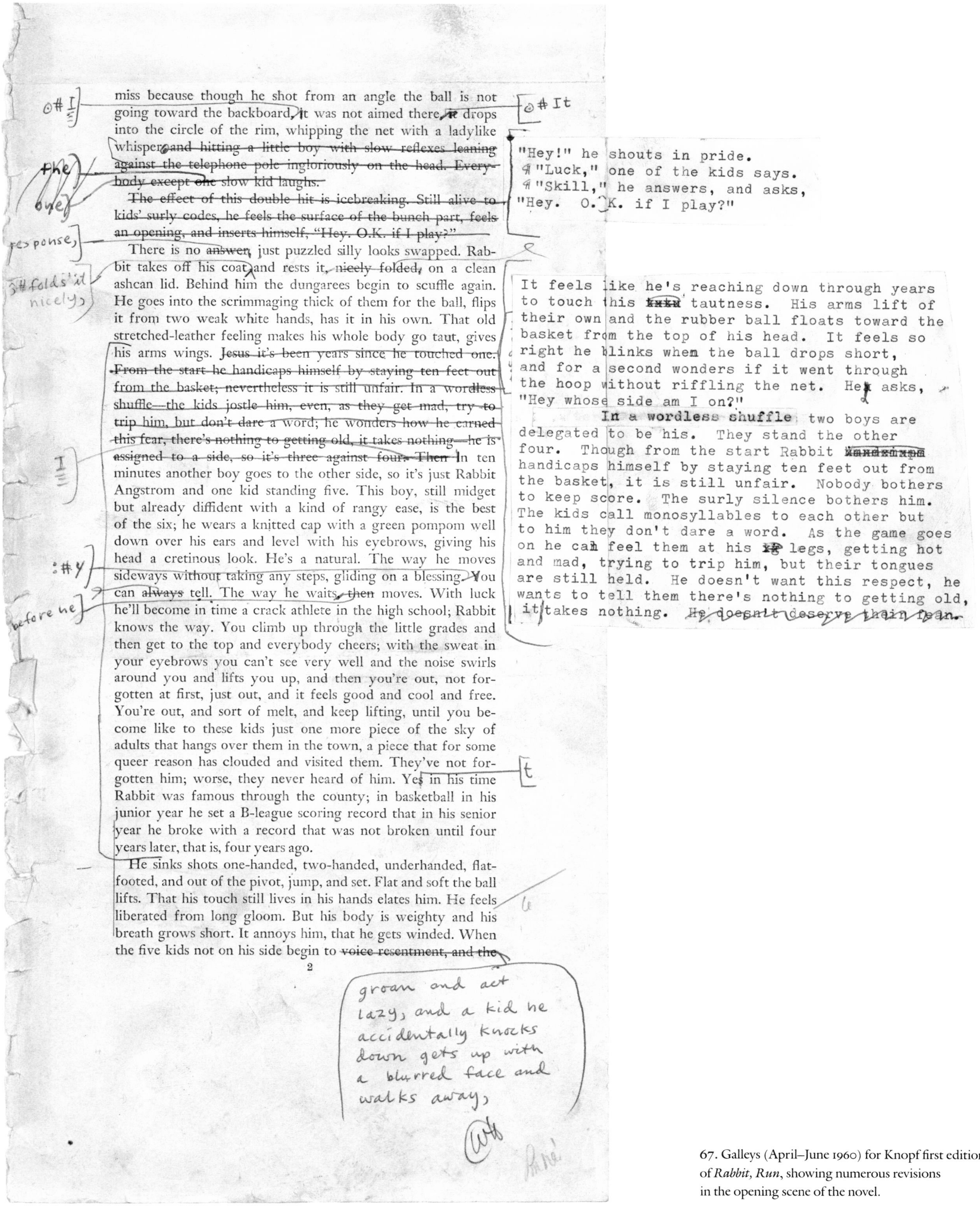

miss because though he shot from an angle the ball is not going toward the backboard, it was not aimed there, it drops into the circle of the rim, whipping the net with a ladylike whisper and hitting a little boy with slow reflexes leaning against the telephone pole ingloriously on the head. Everybody except one slow kid laughs.

The effect of this double hit is icebreaking. Still alive to kids' surly codes, he feels the surface of the bunch part, feels an opening, and inserts himself, "Hey. O.K. if I play?"

There is no answer, just puzzled silly looks swapped. Rabbit takes off his coat and rests it, nicely folded, on a clean ashcan lid. Behind him the dungarees begin to scuffle again. He goes into the scrimmaging thick of them for the ball, flips it from two weak white hands, has it in his own. That old stretched-leather feeling makes his whole body go taut, gives his arms wings. Jesus it's been years since he touched one. From the start he handicaps himself by staying ten feet out from the basket; nevertheless it is still unfair. In a wordless shuffle—the kids jostle him, even, as they get mad, try to trip him, but don't dare a word; he wonders how he earned this fear, there's nothing to getting old, it takes nothing—he is assigned to a side, so it's three against four. Then In ten minutes another boy goes to the other side, so it's just Rabbit Angstrom and one kid standing five. This boy, still midget but already diffident with a kind of rangy ease, is the best of the six; he wears a knitted cap with a green pompom well down over his ears and level with his eyebrows, giving his head a cretinous look. He's a natural. The way he moves sideways without taking any steps, gliding on a blessing. You can always tell. The way he waits, then moves. With luck he'll become in time a crack athlete in the high school; Rabbit knows the way. You climb up through the little grades and then get to the top and everybody cheers; with the sweat in your eyebrows you can't see very well and the noise swirls around you and lifts you up, and then you're out, not forgotten at first, just out, and it feels good and cool and free. You're out, and sort of melt, and keep lifting, until you become like to these kids just one more piece of the sky of adults that hangs over them in the town, a piece that for some queer reason has clouded and visited them. They've not forgotten him; worse, they never heard of him. Yes in his time Rabbit was famous through the county; in basketball in his junior year he set a B-league scoring record that in his senior year he broke with a record that was not broken until four years later, that is, four years ago.

He sinks shots one-handed, two-handed, underhanded, flatfooted, and out of the pivot, jump, and set. Flat and soft the ball lifts. That his touch still lives in his hands elates him. He feels liberated from long gloom. But his body is weighty and his breath grows short. It annoys him, that he gets winded. When the five kids not on his side begin to voice resentment, and the

2

"Hey!" he shouts in pride.
"Luck," one of the kids says.
"Skill," he answers, and asks, "Hey. O.K. if I play?"

It feels like he's reaching down through years to touch this tautness. His arms lift of their own and the rubber ball floats toward the basket from the top of his head. It feels so right he blinks when the ball drops short, and for a second wonders if it went through the hoop without riffling the net. He asks, "Hey whose side am I on?"

In a wordless shuffle two boys are delegated to be his. They stand the other four. Though from the start Rabbit handicaps himself by staying ten feet out from the basket, it is still unfair. Nobody bothers to keep score. The surly silence bothers him. The kids call monosyllables to each other but to him they don't dare a word. As the game goes on he can feel them at his legs, getting hot and mad, trying to trip him, but their tongues are still held. He doesn't want this respect, he wants to tell them there's nothing to getting old, it takes nothing. He doesn't deserve their fear.

groan and act lazy, and a kid he accidentally knocks down gets up with a blurred face and walks away,

67. Galleys (April–June 1960) for Knopf first edition of *Rabbit, Run*, showing numerous revisions in the opening scene of the novel.

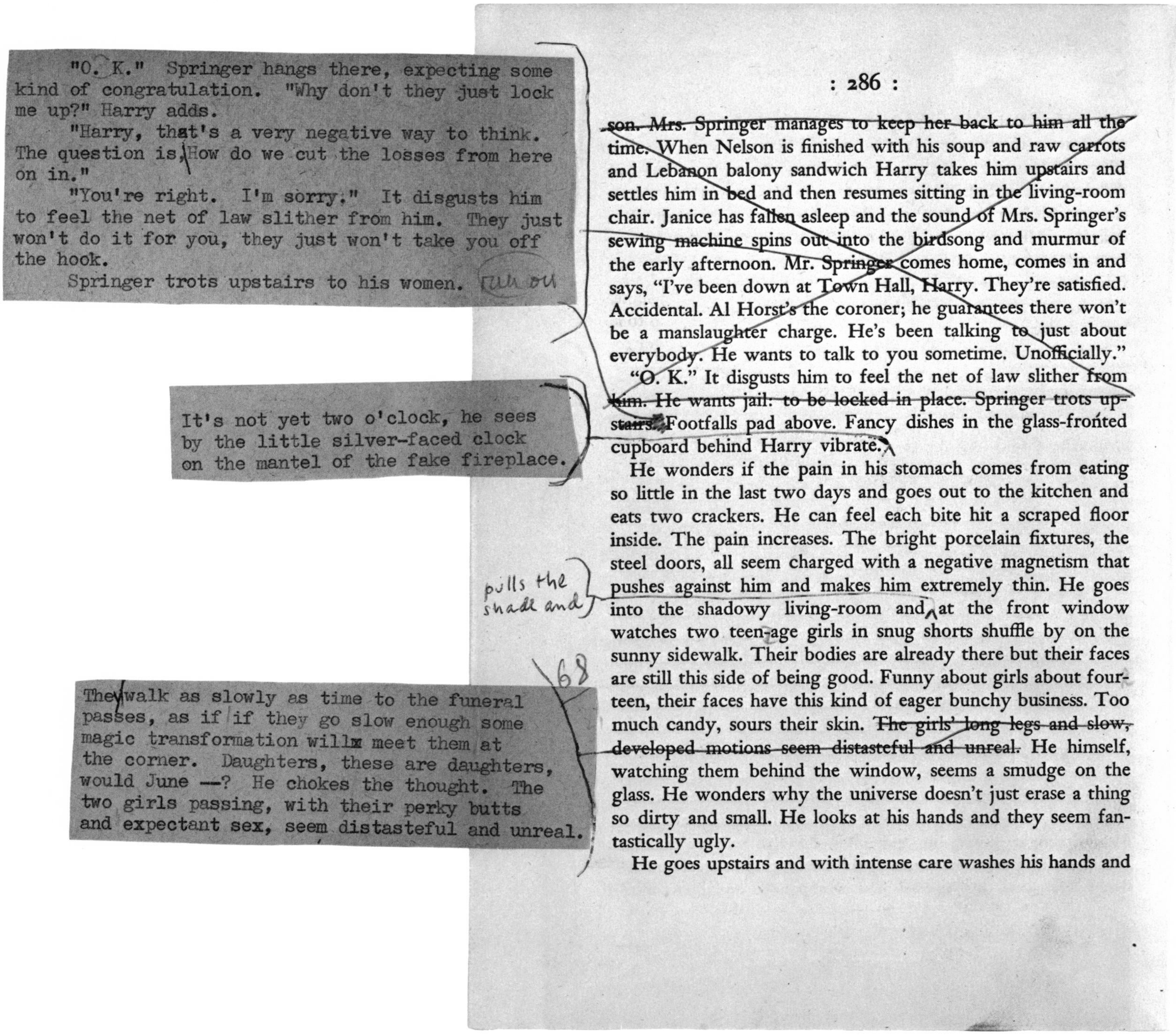

"O. K." Springer hangs there, expecting some kind of congratulation. "Why don't they just lock me up?" Harry adds.

"Harry, that's a very negative way to think. The question is, How do we cut the losses from here on in."

"You're right. I'm sorry." It disgusts him to feel the net of law slither from him. They just won't do it for you, they just won't take you off the hook.

Springer trots upstairs to his women.

It's not yet two o'clock, he sees by the little silver-faced clock on the mantel of the fake fireplace.

pulls the shade and

68

They walk as slowly as time to the funeral passes, as if if they go slow enough some magic transformation willx meet them at the corner. Daughters, these are daughters, would June —? He chokes the thought. The two girls passing, with their perky butts and expectant sex, seem distasteful and unreal.

: 286 :

~~son. Mrs. Springer manages to keep her back to him all the time.~~ When Nelson is finished with his soup and raw carrots and Lebanon balony sandwich Harry takes him upstairs and settles him in bed and then resumes sitting in the living-room chair. Janice has fallen asleep and the sound of Mrs. Springer's sewing machine spins out into the birdsong and murmur of the early afternoon. Mr. Springer comes home, comes in and says, "I've been down at Town Hall, Harry. They're satisfied. Accidental. Al Horst's the coroner; he guarantees there won't be a manslaughter charge. He's been talking to just about everybody. He wants to talk to you sometime. Unofficially."

"O. K." It disgusts him to feel the net of law slither from ~~him. He wants jail: to be locked in place. Springer trots upstairs.~~ Footfalls pad above. Fancy dishes in the glass-fronted cupboard behind Harry vibrate.

He wonders if the pain in his stomach comes from eating so little in the last two days and goes out to the kitchen and eats two crackers. He can feel each bite hit a scraped floor inside. The pain increases. The bright porcelain fixtures, the steel doors, all seem charged with a negative magnetism that pushes against him and makes him extremely thin. He goes into the shadowy living-room and at the front window watches two teen-age girls in snug shorts shuffle by on the sunny sidewalk. Their bodies are already there but their faces are still this side of being good. Funny about girls about fourteen, their faces have this kind of eager bunchy business. Too much candy, sours their skin. ~~The girls' long legs and slow, developed motions seem distasteful and unreal.~~ He himself, watching them behind the window, seems a smudge on the glass. He wonders why the universe doesn't just erase a thing so dirty and small. He looks at his hands and they seem fantastically ugly.

He goes upstairs and with intense care washes his hands and

72. The Deutsch 1961 edition of *Rabbit, Run*, with revisions for the 1964 Penguin edition.